Hudson Valley UFOs

Written by
Linda Zimmermann

To contact the author, email: lindazim@optonline.net

Website: www.gotozim.com

Or write to:

Linda Zimmermann
P.O. Box 192
Blooming Grove, NY 10914

Other UFO Books by Linda Zimmermann:
In the Night Sky: Hudson Valley UFO Sightings from the 1930s to the Present

For more information on the award-winning documentary film,
In the Night Sky, go to: www.nightskyufo.com

To contact C. Burns to report sightings in Pine Bush, NY:
Email: pbmysteries@aol.com
Archive Website: www.pinebushanomaly.com

Title page artwork by Felix Olivieri www.bigguymedia.com

Eagle Press, New York
ISBN: 978-1-937174-01-9

CONTENTS

Introduction

I Never Stopped

This is my second book on UFO sightings in the Hudson River Valley region of New York. Research for my first book, *In the Night Sky* (2013), was an amazing journey. As I was interviewing eyewitnesses and following leads throughout the area, Felix and Sarah Olivieri of Big Guy Media were filming me every step of the way. Their documentary, *In the Night Sky: I Recall a UFO*, was the result.

At the end of February, 2013, Felix and I went to the International UFO Congress in Arizona, and the documentary was entered in their film festival, which was attended by thousands of people. *In the Night Sky* won the People's Choice Award—by a landslide!—and we knew that there was great interest not only in the stories from the Hudson Valley, but also in the way we presented those stories.

In the past year, the success of the film and book has led to other film festivals, radio and television interviews, and many speaking engagements. And with each appearance, more people came forward with new stories. The ink was hardly dry in the first book when it looked like there would be a second book.

It's not that I returned to writing about Unidentified Flying Objects, it's that I never stopped! People just kept calling, writing, and emailing me to ask if my first book was completed, yet even though I told them it was finished, they gave me their stories anyway. And I'm glad they did, because it inspired my research to move in several new directions.

For example, because of a connection I made at the Pine Bush UFO Festival, a gentleman told me his story about an incident at Stewart Air Force base in the 1960s. That led me to look into Stewart sightings reported in Project Blue Book, which led to an entire chapter of Blue Book sightings throughout the Hudson Valley. That, in turn, prompted a lengthy newspaper archive search which uncovered sightings from over a century ago!

All of this proves to me that the Hudson Valley is most likely the #1 Hotspot for UFO activity in the country. Yet, I have found that even UFO enthusiasts living in the region don't know about the long and varied history of sightings. Unfortunately, I've also found that many people across the country never even heard of the Hudson Valley!

I hope to change that.

If you have any interest in the UFO field, you need to know about the more than 100 years of sightings in this area. You need to know about the "mysterious airships," the disks, the triangles, and the rectangles. You need to know about the close encounters and missing time, and the mass sightings. There are mysteries here that need to be solved.

There are UFOs in the Hudson Valley.

Linda Zimmermann
January 2014

Acknowledgements

Thanks to C. Burns for his continued efforts in the field of Pine Bush UFO research, as well as his help with my projects. Thanks also to Ginny for her support and generosity in making her property available for stakeouts.

As always, many thanks to my husband, Bob Strong, for his editorial assistance, and for not only tolerating, but enjoying all my crazy ideas. (At least I think so?)

I greatly appreciate the kindness and expertise of chemist Phyllis Budinger, who shed light on an old mystery.

And to the people of the Hudson Valley, who never cease to amaze me with the number and variety of their personal UFO experiences.

1
1909: The Mysterious Airships

Most UFO enthusiasts have heard of the "Mysterious Airship" wave of sightings in the United States during 1896-97, with the strange craft being spotted from California to Texas. Given the state of aviation at the time—it would be six years before the Wright Brothers first powered flight—there is no suitable explanation for the craft and lights seen in the night skies across so many states during those two years.

What is less known, and equally inexplicable, is the wave of mysterious airship sightings in the northeast in 1909-10. Many of those sightings occurred in the Hudson Valley, as is evidenced by this article in the August 1, 1909 edition of the New York newspaper, *The Sun*:

MYSTERIOUS AIRSHIP

It Flies Only at Night and Keeps Orange County Folks Up Watching It

MIDDLETOWN, N.Y., July 31--A mysterious airship which flies only at night is causing considerable excitement and keeping the people of Orange county residing between Goshen and Newburgh up nights in their efforts to get a look at it. For the last month persons who have been out late nights have reported seeing an airship, but few believed the stories. For a week or more the flying machine had not been seen, but at 11 o'clock last night it made its appearance near Goshen. It was flying high in the air and carried a light which first attracted attention. It flew very fast and was last seen traveling in the direction of Newburgh.

Those who have seen the machine say it is shaped like a balloon and has wings on each side and a cigar shaped car underneath. The sound of a motor was distinctly heard by those who saw the machine.

While the description sounds like something out of Jules Verne, or just a conglomeration of the characteristics of a balloon, dirigible, and an airplane, I am suspicious about the reliability of this aspect of the article, as all the sightings in the northeast were at night (this one also states it was 11pm), and all of the other witnesses said it was invariably too dark to see the actual craft. At best, people were seeing the light (or lights) and a dark shape. In any event, this article certainly caught my attention, and I knew I had to do some more digging.

After conducting an extensive search of newspaper archives, I came across several other articles relating to this wave of sightings—including several things that made fun of what people claimed to see in a variety of ways that were remarkably similar to the critical reactions to more modern UFO sightings. To my amazement, I soon realized that here were all the elements of denials, ridiculous excuses, hoaxers, and belittled witnesses already in place, more than 100 years ago!

Before getting into all the details, however, it's important to give some background on what the state of aviation was in 1909. As a picture is worth a thousand words, here's a photo of the U.S. Army's first airplane, purchased from the Wright Brothers in 1909 for the huge sum of $30,000. It could fly at an average speed of 42 miles per hour, which was very fast for that time, and could safely fly for about an hour. Unfortunately, safety was a relative term, as it turned out to be far better at crashing than flying.

It's also *very important* to note that the vast majority of the mysterious airship sightings in 1909 were at night, and *no airplanes had yet flown at night in the United States,* or anywhere else in the world. In fact, the *very first night flight on record was not until 1910,* and it took place in Buenos Aires, Argentina.

So essentially, in 1909 in the United States, there were very few planes, they *only flew in daylight,* they couldn't go much faster than 40 miles per hour, and they couldn't fly much longer than an hour. So what did that leave in the skies over America? Unpowered balloons at the mercy of the winds, and dirigibles. Certainly, the master of dirigibles was Count Ferdinand von Zeppelin, and in 1909 his LZ-4 was the best available. The LZ-4 could go 30 mph and had stayed aloft an impressive 31 hours.

However, *all the Zeppelins were in Germany,* and the United States had only a rather pathetic version of an airship owned by the Army Signal Corps, known as the SC-1. It could only manage 20 mph, and stayed in the air for just two hours.

LZ-4 ZEPPELIN
MAX. SPEED: 30MPH
ENDURANCE: 31 HOURS

SC-1: SPEED 20MPH
ENDURANCE: 2 HOURS

3

With these facts in mind, consider the following article which appeared in the *Newburgh Daily Journal*, July 26, 1909:

"AIR SHIP" IS SEEN AGAIN FROM WASHINGTON HEIGHTS
SHE WAS SWOOPING

Too Dark, It Is Said, to Discern Outlines of the "Ship."

About 10:30 o'clock Sunday night several Newburghers in Washington Heights observed the much-talked-about airship rise above the Fishkill mountains at a point deemed to be in line with the (illegible) Beacon. While the night was too dark to discern the outlines of the machine, it was of considerable length (illegible) a light was plainly visible at (illegible) end, and these two lights were (illegible) considerable distance apart.

Spy glasses were procured by the observers on the Heights and the gradual rising of one (illegible) above the level of the other gave (illegible) that the machine was "swooping" in its motions. The "air-ship" gradually arose, but did not seem to be going either away from or coming toward the observers in Newburgh. But its motion was gradually higher and higher until at 11:30 the machine seemed to be almost twice as high above the mountains as the top of the mountains seems to be above the level of the river. [Note: That would give an altitude of about 4500 feet.]

When the observers ceased watching the movements of the "air-ship" at 11:30 it was at its highest point, and seemed to be going higher. The alternate rising of one of the two lights above the other suggested that the movements of the apparatus were "rolling like a ship, or swooping" like a bird.

Here's another article from the *Poughkeepsie Daily Eagle*, on August 24, 1909:

Apropos of the statement of several people in Newburgh and Fishkill and also in Poughkeepsie that they have seen a mysterious airship floating around over head at night, we find the following in the Rochester

4

Democrat Chronicle, which shows that this peculiar form of hallucination is not confined to the valley of the Hudson: "Mysterious airships and aeroplanes are beginning to fly through the darkness of the night in various parts of the country. Nobody knows whither they come or whither they go. Apparently they start from nowhere and never land. Perhaps they are the advance couriers of that anticipated comet due here some time next winter or spring. It is clearly absurd to believe that so conspicuous an object as a dirigible balloon or even an aeroplane capable of carrying two men could be assembled, inflated, started and handled without attracting the attention of the omnipresent agents of the newspaper. We may add to this that so far we know the people who think they have seen the mysterious airship in this locality have declared that it always carries a light. In fact, it is the light they have been seeing. They are unable to tell whether it was a dirigible balloon or an aeroplane that was carrying it, although on several occasions this mysterious visitor was reported on moonlight nights. Now there is no law yet compelling airships to carry lights, no reason to suppose that they do carry lights and, in fact, we have the statement of one of the leading aeropilots that no aeroplane in this country has yet made a night flight. (text illegible) *to see the Hudson-Fulton[1] flight, if it ever occurs, but we hope by that time at least some fliers will be able to fly in the broad day time.*

This last article has many things worth noting:
- We see that in the Hudson Valley, the airships were not only being seen from Goshen to Newburgh, but across the river in Fishkill and as far north as Poughkeepsie, roughly an overall distance of about 40 miles.
- The reporter is referring to these sightings as a "peculiar form of hallucination"—clearly disparaging the witnesses.

---

[1] The Hudson-Fulton flight was made by Wilbur Wright October 4, 1909, as part of the 300th anniversary of Henry Hudson's voyage up the river, and the centennial celebration of Fulton's steamboat. A million people watched as Wright flew 20 miles in 33 minutes, going up the Hudson River from Governors Island to Grant's Tomb and back. Due to the unreliable nature of aircraft at the time, he had lashed a canoe to the bottom of his airplane just in case he crashed into the river!

- The reporter states that, "Nobody knows whither they come or whither they go. Apparently they start from nowhere and never land." Certainly sounds like a UFO!
- The reporter also suggests that these airships may be "the advance couriers of that anticipated comet," which hopefully was meant in jest, as it's simply too ludicrous to relate unidentified aircraft with an approaching comet.
- The reporter does make an excellent point about it being "clearly absurd to believe that so conspicuous an object as a dirigible balloon or even an aeroplane capable of carrying two men could be assembled, inflated, started and handled without attracting the attention of the omnipresent agents of the newspaper." In addition to the fact that such secrecy would be next to impossible, it would also be very hard to believe that if someone had managed to build such a superior vehicle—capable of high speeds and night flights—they wouldn't have tried to cash in on it, as there were fortunes to be made with aircraft.
- Finally, there is the pilot's testimony that "there is no law yet compelling airships to carry lights, no reason to suppose that they do carry lights and, in fact, we have the statement of one of the leading aeropilots that no aeroplane in this country has yet made a night flight."

As I was scanning reel after reel of old newspapers on microfilm—which kind of makes me cross-eyed and seasick if I do it too long or too fast—my eye just happened to catch a tiny paragraph at the bottom of a page of the *Goshen Democrat* from August 5, 1909 with the title "Human Volcano Erupts." Thinking it would be something funny, I stopped scanning and enlarged that section. I was both amused and delighted by the nature of the brief article, and the fact that it *was* actually related to the mysterious airships!

Human Volcano Erupts.

Otto Pushman, Newburgh's champion cusser, had been sent to jail for thirty days for using sulphurous language. During the nocturnal hours of Tuesday he was discovered on Grand street looking for that ding-blasted airship that the Newburgh papers tell about and cursing fervently at the blankety-blanked moon.

This might just be the first—and only—case in history where someone was put in jail for swearing at a UFO, and one he didn't even get to see! This also reminded me of the people in Pine Bush in the 1980s and 90s who were threatened with arrest when they made "skywatching" illegal, although it was Otto Pushman's "sulphorous language" and not his standing on the street and watching the sky that landed him in jail for an entire month.

The mysterious Hudson Valley airship sightings spread throughout New England by the end of December. Many thousands of witnesses watched in amazement as something with lights circled, hovered, and sped off into the darkness. The following is a report from Rhode Island which appeared in the *New York Tribune*:

SEEING THINGS AT NIGHT
Watchers of Providence Tell of Illuminated Flying Machines
(By Telegraph to The Tribune)
Providence, Dec. 21.—People in this section who were out at 1:15 this morning were attracted by the mysterious airship which went over the city of Pawtucket and the outlying districts of Providence, going in the direction of Newport.

Two red lights in the sky first appeared, and it became evident that they were gradually proceeding southward. Among those who saw the aerial navigator was Mrs. William S. Forsythe, of No. 85 Evergreen street, Pawtucket. All were able to make out the outline of the flying machine against the background of stars.

The airship was then seen the next night over Worcester and Marlboro, MA.

AIRSHIP STIRS CITY
Twice Appears Over Worcester—Tillinghast Suspected

Worcester, Mass., Dec 22.—Flying through the night at an avergae speed of from thirty to forty miles an hour, a mysterious airship to-night appeared over Worcester, hovered over the city a few minutes, disappeared for about two hours and then returned to cut four circles above the gaping city, meanwhile sweeping the heavens with a searchlight of very high power. The news of its presence spread like wildfire and thousands thronged the streets to watch the mysterious visitor.

The airship remained over the city for about fifteen minutes, all the time at a height that most observers set at about two thousand feet, too far to enable even its precise shape to be seen. After a time it dispperaed in the direction of Marlboro, only to return later.

Coming up from the southeast, the sky voyager veered to the west, remained in sight a few moments, and then disappered to the northwest. In five minutes the searchlight was again seen glowing in the distance like a monster star, and the ship came up, hovered over the city a short time, and disappeared to the southeast.

Two hours later an eager shout from the waiting crowds announced its return. Slowly, its light sweeping the heavens it circled four times above the city and then disappeared, and finally heading first southerly and then to the east.

At the time of the airship visit Wallace E. Tillinghast, the Worcester man who recently claimed to have invented a marvellous aeroplane in which he said he journeyed to New York and return by way of Boston, was absent from his home and could not be located.

8

Marlboro, Mass, Dec. 22.—An airship was sighted over Marlboro early tonight, going northwest at thirty or more miles an hour. Persons in all sections of the city reported having had a glimpse of it. Its general course, they say, was in the direction of Clinton.

Again, we can rule out airplanes because, as was stated earlier, they did not fly at night and could not fly for hours at the time. The finest Zeppelins may have been capable of the duration of these sightings, but not at speeds of 40 mph and above, and, most importantly, there were no Zeppelins in the country. As American dirigibles were inferior to the German Zeppelins, these mysterious airships were not of domestic origin either. Over the past century, many aviation experts have confirmed that no one had yet built anything that had all of the flight capabilities of these nocturnal airships of 1909.

Which doesn't mean someone didn't try to claim that he had produced such an amazing airship.

Enter businessman Wallace E. Tillinghast (mentioned in the above article), the hoaxer every good UFO wave seems to require to muddy the waters of legitimate research. In mid-December, Tillighast made the outlandish claim that he had invented a heavier-than-air flying machine that could attain unheard of speeds of 120 mph, carry three people, and travel at least 300 miles without refueling.

He also claimed that he had already made over one hundred flights, including an incredible nighttime journey from Worcester to New York City, circling the Statue of Liberty four times at an altitude of 4,000 feet, and then passing through Boston on his way home. During that alleged flight, the aircraft's engine cut out, but he managed to keep the plane gliding for over 45 minutes while his two mechanics fixed the engine in mid-air!

As there had been sightings of mysterious airships throughout the Hudson Valley during the summer, and then subsequent sightings throughout New England, people actually believed the outrageous claims. However, as days and weeks passed without Tillinghast ever publicly producing his remarkable vehicle, it soon became evident he was lying. Unfortunately, even though he was proven to be a fraud, he left a mark on this wave of sightings that is still haunting UFO researchers to this day.

Once the lies were revealed, the same newspapers who had sung the praises of the airship's spectacular feats of aviation seen by countless reliable witnesses such as judges, professors, teachers, and policemen, now said that all of the witnesses had only seen the planet Venus, or "fire balloons."

Modern-day UFO skeptics now twist the facts and say that the mysterious airship sightings of 1909 occurred only *after* Tillinghast made his December announcement, so they are either ignorant of the Hudson Valley sightings five months earlier, or are simply choosing to ignore them. Therefore, they say, the tens of thousands of witnesses were simply suffering from "mass hysteria" and "mass delusions."

A cartoon in the *New York Press* on December 27, 1909 was already poking fun at these witnesses and sightings (see previous page). As if excuses such as mass hysteria and Santa Claus weren't demeaning enough, there was this mention in the *New York Daily News* on September 3, 1910:

Citizens of New York City are recovering from their panic. The mysterious airship turns out to have been a kite, flown for the amusement of a six-year-old youngster.

England also had its own wave of nighttime airship sightings in 1909. Due to the fears of a German invasion, they were dubbed Scareships, and spread panic throughout the public. No suitable explanation for these sightings has ever been found, either, so naturally, that wave has also been classified as the result of mass hysteria.

So here we have it, the tried and true formula for dealing with unexplained aerial phenomena, whether it was a hundred years ago or recent activity:

1909 Mysterious Airships = Hoaxer+Kite+Balloons+Venus+Mass Hysteria / Newspaper Ridicule

1950s Flying Saucers = Secret Military Aircraft+Hoaxers with Pie Pans on Strings+Weather Balloons+Venus+Mass Hysteria/Newspaper Ridcule

1980s Hudson Valley Triangles = Secret Military Aircraft+Hoaxers with Ultralight Planes+Venus+Mass Hysteria/Newspaper and Television Ridicule

21st Century Sightings = Secret Military Aircraft+Photoshop and Video Hoaxers+Venus+Mass Hysteria / Multimedia Ridicule

I think it's important to note that no one during the 1909 wave was claiming that the lighted objects they were seeing in the night sky were alien spacecraft. Aviation was in its infancy and it was an exciting time of invention and discovery, so the mysterious airships were seen with fascination and the expectation that the inventor would be stepping forward at any moment. Witnesses simply had no reason to lie about what they were seeing, and had no mass delusions of an extraterrestrial invasion.

Here are the basic facts:

- Large aircraft with bright lights were traveling at night at speeds and over distances not possible by any aircraft in the country in 1909.
- While some claimed to hear engine sounds or a soft "whirring," others had trouble believing their own eyes because the mysterious airships were silent.
- People watched in facsination for hours because they knew they were seeing something far beyond the current known technology, but never considered it to be extraterrestrial.
- There are estimates that tens of thousands of people saw these lighted craft at night from New York to Maine in 1909-10.
- Over one hundred years of research has not turned up one shred of evidence of any advanced aircraft built in 1909—no inventors, no blueprints, no prototypes or models, and definitely no aircraft.

So what were these mysterious airships and what does it all mean? Given all of the facts, the wave of 1909-10 is just further proof that the Hudson Valley *was, and is*, the country's #1 Hotspot for UFO activity.

2
Triangles, Boomerangs, and Vs

Scott, Brewster, NY, 1970s and 1983

Scott was too young remember his fist UFO sighting in the 1970s. He was in the car with his mother, and they were driving on Route 684 near Brewster. There were strange lights in the sky, but they weren't close enough to see the body of the craft.

However, he vividly remembers his sighting on the night of March 17, 1983—one of the most famous nights in Hudson Valley UFO history. That was the night that hundreds, and perhaps thousands, of people saw a massive, silent boomerang or triangular-shaped craft hovering above Route 84 in Brewster. One of those witnesses was Dennis Sant, who would later be featured on the show *Unsolved Mysteries*, as well as in my book *In the Night Sky*. Scott was close friends with one of Dennis' sons, and he lived just a short distance away, on the other (south) side of Route 84.

Scott's parents were out that night, and he was home watching television. He kept noticing some "funny lights" through the drapes, and got up several times wondering what kind of aircraft it was. As it got closer, he quickly realized this was nothing he had ever seen before. He ran toward the front door, stepped outside and "stood in awe" of what was directly above his house.

"It was a mammoth, solid structure, triangular, silent, and hovering just above the trees. It had to be two or three football fields long. It was so low if I had a tennis racket and ball and could have hit it. I ran inside to call a friend nearby, but by the time he went outside it was gone."

Scott admits he was "a little bit paralyzed" by the incredible sight, which lasted between five to ten minutes, but he didn't have any fear. The overwhelming feeling he had was one of "exhilaration." In fact, he admits that "it was a letdown" when it never came back.

"I really can't convey the feelings I had that night, like this was a once in a lifetime thing."

Ed Mulvaney, Hopewell Junction, NY, Summer 1979

In December of 2013, I received the following email. This was of particular interest to me, because as Ed points out, it is a very early sighting of a triangular-shaped craft, occurring three years before the main wave of sightings of this type in this area.

Don't know if you're still interested in these sightings, but I have witnessed one of these huge craft from a distance and from right underneath. The main thing that confuses me is the fact I saw this in the summer of 1979. All the accounts I have read or saw in the media talks about 1982.

I was heading west on Route 84 late one evening coming down Stormville Mountain when I noticed a huge craft about 1/2 a mile or so away moving east in the same direction as I was. I drove and watched it until I exited north onto the Taconic State Parkway. As I entered northbound about a 1/4 mile up was an old gas station at the first crossroad you come to. I saw maybe 15 or 20 cars pulled over. I pulled over onto the left shoulder behind another parked car and walked over to a group of people just as this craft came into view. It was mostly a wooded area, but open along the parkway so we had a fair amount of sky to see it pass right over us just above the tree tops.

It was triangular, and the size was just unbelievable. It was as large as a new cruise ship. When it passed over it blocked out most of the stars, and because it was moving as slow as it was, it took a good 20 to 30 seconds to completely pass over.

What struck me as it passed were two things. There was no sound from this craft, but a small single-engine Cessna-type aircraft was north of us maybe 3 or 4 miles and I could distinctly hear the drone from its motor. Looking at the underside of this huge silent craft, I had noticed a ring of changing color lights that looked like they were pulsating and chasing around an oval-shaped protrusion that was in the center of the craft. The craft body looked to be a dark grey/black metal that had structures like support beams. At the tips of the triangular-shaped craft were bright white lights that stayed on with one intensity.

The craft then passed over the northern tree line and went out of sight. I remember saying to one of the people standing around mostly silent,

"What did we just see?" I don't remember him replying. It was surreal. Within a minute everyone got back into their cars and drove off. I still have dreams of this. It was a profound moment in my life. Until then I was neither a skeptic nor a believer, but that has changed. I know deep down what I saw was not from this planet.

Thanks for reading my experience.

Kingston, NY, c. 1981-83

This is a fascinating case due to both the quality of the eyewitness account, and the profession of the eyewitness. In June of 2013, I received the following email:

"I saw in an article from last year that you were seeking witnesses to the triangular UFO. I saw it with my own eyes for about 10-15 minutes. I can't recall the date (I'd guess some time in the '81 to '83 time frame), but I do recall the incident and what I saw very well. Please let me know if you're still interested in this."

I responded to "John" that I was interested, and asked his to describe his experience in as much detail as possible:

Okay, I'll do my best.

I would guess I was about 15 or 16 years old and was hanging out with some friends near the railroad tracks behind Spiegel Bros. paper company (678 Ulster Ave., Kingston, NY) when we saw lights in the sky coming over the tree line. We immediately became interested because it was unlike anything we had ever seen before. The lights were in the shape of a flock of geese (best way I can describe it) and I think were white, green, and red. Some of the lights were larger than others. I believe the lights changed colors while we were observing the object. It moved very slowly through the sky and we were amazed by the fact that we could hear absolutely no sound. I believe the lights outlined the shape of the object but it was very hard to tell because the area inside the lights was so dark. I am confident that it was solid between the lights and can tell you positively that this was not a group of ultralight planes or anything like that as I think some have posited. I'm absolutely convinced this was a single object. I remember finding it very difficult to tell how high the object was in the sky, but it didn't seem to be more than 1000 feet up or so. It was very, very large.

So, I and a friend stood mesmerized watching this thing. The other two friends who were with us grew frightened and left the scene. I found it a bit frightening as well, but I was so intrigued that I actually wanted to follow it when it moved away about 10 minutes later. The most remarkable part of the experience was when the object completely stopped moving immediately above us and hovered in one place for 3 minutes or so. It was virtually silent, although when it was hovering right above us I thought I may have heard a barely-perceptible hum. I had the distinct feeling as it hovered above us that it was studying us as intently as we were studying it, and I even sensed that a very faint light was being shined down at us, perhaps with a faint red color. I can't say for sure if this was some kind of spotlight or just one of the lights from the object, but it felt to me at the time like it was being directed at us. I remember my heart racing and the thrilling (but also a bit frightening) feeling in those few minutes while the object hovered in one place above us. Eventually, it started moving away slowly toward the tree line and then I remember it moving much more quickly to the northeast (basically in the direction of Ulster Landing Park) and the Hudson River and disappearing.

I should mention to you that I'm definitely not a "loony-bird." I'm a respected professional and I've only shared this story with a few very close family members. I'm a natural born skeptic and don't believe in ghosts, spirits, fate, karma, life after death or anything else that can't be proven by science. However I do believe what I see with my own eyes, and this really did happen! When I started Googling UFOs in the Hudson Valley recently I was astounded by what I found. It's good to know that so many people saw what I saw. I'd love to know if you've come across any explanations and/or how my experience was similar to or different than what you've heard from others.

I'm pretty sure the Kingston Freeman published a story or two about this when it happened, so that might be a good way to try to pinpoint the date.

Hope this helps

As John was obviously an educated professional, I asked him if he wouldn't mind telling what he did. Turns out, he is an attorney and law

16

professor, and a skeptical one, at that! This is clearly a man who lives by facts and incontrovertible proof.

While I don't know if this case would hold up in a court of law—although cases have been won with less than four eyewitnesses—it is clear that for John, the existence of this massive V-shaped craft is beyond a reasonable doubt.

One of the things I always ask witnesses is if they ever had any other sightings, and how the experiences influenced their lives. John offered the following:

"No sightings for me before or since. Just that one amazing night that left such an impression on me that I often find myself thinking about it and trying to explain it three decades later."

Laura, Yonkers, NY, Late 1980s

It has been many years since my UFO experience. So long, in fact, that the day and year have become a blur. I was about 20 years old at the time. On a partly cloudy day in the late 1980s in Yonkers, NY, I was driving north on the Sprain Brook Parkway when I noticed in the distance ahead an airplane was flying very low. The first thought that came to my mind was how unusual it was for a plane to fly that low in this area.

It was far enough away from me that I didn't question what it was. It looked like an airplane. I kept losing it behind the trees as the parkway was winding; then, as I passed the Tuckahoe Road exit I realized the plane was still in view and I was actually catching up to it. How could it be possible to catch up to an airplane traveling in the same direction?

It seemed to be moving about half the speed of my car; so if I was travelling about 60 mph, it seemed to have been traveling about 30 mph. As I approached a stop sign at an exit at Jackson Avenue (boarder of Yonkers and Scarsdale) I was practically underneath it.

This is where I got a good look and it was certainly not an airplane. It was an immense, metallic, boomerang-shaped craft with large white circular lights lining the bottom of it. It seemed to slow down where it appeared to hover, but was actually slowly gliding up the parkway, maybe 50 feet above the treetops, and made absolutely no noise. I couldn't believe what I was seeing so I looked to see if other drivers around me had noticed it too.

Yup, they were also peering out through their windshields. I felt like jumping out of my car and shouting, "Are you seeing that? What is that thing?!" But I didn't, I drove off and went on my way. I watched it through my rearview mirror as I drove away towards Central Avenue. As I approached my turn I kept looking for it, but it had either disappeared through the clouds or took off. I told some family and friends about the sighting, but for the most part I kept it to myself.

At another time, my mom told me of an incident that occurred sometime in the 90s (date unknown) at a power station in Yonkers, which happens to be located adjacent to Tuckahoe Road alongside the Sprain Parkway, not far from my sighting. Apparently, an object was seen hovering over the grid and subsequently resulted in a local blackout.

At another time during the day at home, my mom and uncle had seen something strange in the sky while they were in the backyard. My mom said they saw an object in the sky that looked like a metallic square with one of its corners cut off. My uncle got so scared when he saw it that he ran inside the house. It apparently hovered in the sky over the house, pivoted around several times and then shot out into the sky and disappeared.

Other than that I hadn't heard of any similar sightings in Westchester County and never heard of any boomerang-shaped UFOs being seen either. Over the years, I began to question my experience. I thought this experience could very well have been conjured up by an overactive imagination, so I began to entertain the thought that the whole thing never really happened, until…

Twenty plus years later I happened to be watching an episode of UFO Hunters on television. This particular episode had to do with vortexes and their locations where massive UFO activity had been reported. I was floored when they described the UFO I had seen; boomerang shaped, low flying, silent, lights, 30 mph, traveling north. Apparently, thousands of people have witnessed and reported this throughout the Hudson Valley. Here I thought I was practically alone in this experience, but it turned out to be one of the most common UFO sightings reported in the Hudson Valley region.

I found it interesting, however, that my sighting occurred in the daytime, where all the reports I've read so far were night sightings. I feel privileged to have had such a clear, unobstructed view; I only wish there were smart phones at the time—what amazing photos I could have taken. I'm not sure what I saw, whether it was alien or just us somehow. Either way, I hope to someday learn exactly what I saw that day and why it was there.

Bhavani and Sharath, Mahopac, NY, 1990 & 1992

When Bhavani was a little girl growing up in Singapore, her family would sit outside watching the stars. She remembers looking up and saying, "My people are out there and they left me behind." It's an odd thing for a child to say, but she explained that in the Indian texts like the Ramayana and Bhagavad Gita, they speak of people coming from the sky in vehicles. These texts, along with her feelings of a connection to the stars, made her "culturally prepared" (my term) for what she would see in 1990, and then again in 1992.

Bhavani and her husband, Sharath, moved to Mahopac in 1989. During the summer of 1990, her husband and son were driving a friend home to Briarcliff Manor. On their way home, they saw a huge boomerang-shaped craft in the sky, slowly moving to the northeast. At one point, they were at just the right position and angle to see that there was a window at the front point of the boomerang. They followed the craft for about 12 minutes, and its path brought it within sight of their house.

Sharath ran inside and told Bhavani and their daughter to come out and see the UFO. Rushing outside, they all stood in awe of the enormous craft. On the bottom surface there were red and white lights. The surface was dark, but reflective. It moved extremely slowly, and completely silently. It took about 5 to 8 minutes to move out of sight, making the total time of the sighting an impressive 20 minutes.

"We were not at all scared," Bhavani told me, the excitement still evident in her voice even after all these years. It was a thrilling sight, and one they all hoped to see again that summer. Unfortunately, it did not reappear, nor did it the following summer, even though they were "always looking for it."

Then in the summer of 1992, at about 9:15pm, Bhavani heard her neighbor screaming her name. Racing outside, she found her neighbor standing in the yard in a very agitated state. Before Bhavani could ask what was wrong, the woman yelled, "Look up!"

It was the same boomerang-shaped craft and it was just above treetop height directly over them, "and it was wider than a Boeing 747." While Bhavani was captivated by the incredible sight, her neighbor was not so enthusiastic.

"I just don't like these things!" she shouted, and then ran into her house. She had obviously seen these UFOs before, and they completely unnerved her. Afterwards, she refused to talk about them.

Bhavani also ran, but to tell her family that, "The UFO has come back!"

As it was much closer than it had been in 1990, they were able to see that the metallic surface was dark brown, and reflected the white and red lights. There was "absolutely zero sound" from the craft and "none of the leaves on the trees moved," so it wasn't creating any kind of turbulence as it moved ever so slowly.

"We were all so happy it had returned, we were hoping it would beam us up!" Bhavani explained. "As I stood there, I just felt gratitude that I was able to see it again."

They weren't content with this incredibly close sighting, and as the craft moved away, they grabbed a video camera and jumped into the car to follow it. As Sharath drove, Bhavani did her best to film the massive craft, but it proved impossible. Just when they thought they were lined up to get it on camera, it would travel sideways or make some other maneuver to stay out of range. Disappointed that they didn't get the video evidence they hoped for, the entire family was nonetheless elated by this second sighting.

While neither of these events made it into the local newspapers, they later found out that other neighbors had witnessed this same boomerang, and many people around Lake Mahopac had sightings over the years. Bhavani told me they were going to make it their "summer project" to see more UFOs, and part of that plan will be to sleep out on the porch every night. She feels that she will have another sighting, possibly this year. And if she does, with any luck, maybe she won't be left behind this time?

Scott Elder, Greenwood Lake, NY
May 23, 1993, 9pm

I live on the west shore of Greenwood Lake on the north end of the lake. I have large windows facing to the east; I overlook the lake and look at the ridge on the east side of the lake. I was watching TV on this evening when I noticed a bright light over the ridge to the east.

I have flown corporate jets for over 20 years now—started in 1987, and I know most of the New York flight patterns as far as departure and arrival routes. The only airplanes that depart this far north going west bound are typically LaGuardia or Teterboro departures going to Buffalo or Green Bay, or Minneapolis, etc. The Chicago routes are further south over Morristown and such, so this area is pretty quiet for departures.

So I saw this bright light over the ridge to the east out of the corner of my eye and said to myself "a LaGuardia departure," as they come towards my house in the climb with the white "recognition light" they use at low altitude. Typically, the light goes out eventually (either 10000 or 18000ft on policy), the aircraft is then over my house and that's when you finally hear the engines at climb power.

Well, I go back to watching TV, and a few minutes later I realize I've heard no engine noise. I glance to my left, and the bright white light is still over the ridge to my east. So I watch it for a bit and realize it's been in the same spot for over 5 minutes. I finally get off of the couch and go over to the sliding door. I stand there and watch the light for another minute or two, and notice it's exceedingly bright and twinkling a bit. I pick up the binoculars I keep on a hook, and look at the object. I then realize that there are 3 very bright white lights, one at the top and two at the bottom in a triangle, and that interspersed among them are flashing lights of many colors—blue, red, orange I remember mostly.

I keep trying to get them to match up with aircraft position lights (red, green, white, and small), aircraft strobes (intense white flashing pulses), aircraft beacons (rotating red on top and bottom), and the bright white recognition light (similar to landing lights but used in flight)...no luck. No matter how I try to make this cluster of lights shape up to be an airplane it just doesn't fit.

By now I've been watching this thing for 5-7 minutes and I start to realize it still hasn't moved. I also try to imagine if it is one large object relatively close to me like a 747, but it would need a light on the nose, and one on each wingtip, and that's not the configuration for recognition lights, and then the little lights don't match up at all, not to mention there is no motion. I mean, it would have been here by now if it were a 747.

I also start thinking ok, maybe its three in formation further away...but that would have to be even east of the Hudson River, and still the lights don't add up...the 3 recognition lights maybe, but then no to the rest of the colored lights, though while dimmer are still very vivid. So about now I open the door, go out on the deck, right to the railing's edge, with the binoculars...there is just no way to explain it...as I watched this thing thru the binoculars I got a very distinct feeling that I wasn't the only one doing the watching...the hairs on my neck started to rise...it's now been close to 10 minutes, and again I'm struggling to determine am I seeing an intermediate-sized object at 2-4 miles away, or a very large object a bit more distant?

With that, the 3 white lights bank 45 degrees to its right (my left) and the object pivots in the relative space of a finger spread at arm's length, continues to its right until it has completed 270 degrees of turn and departs at high speed to my right, headed southbound in a climbing, straight line of 20 degrees or so elevation. Since I'm standing at the railing, I continue to follow it. I have to take four or five quick steps along the railing to keep track of it as it disappears to the south.

The next day I went to work at Teterboro. I was a copilot then, and I sat at the adding machine...I just picked 4 or 5 sample numbers...of how far did I see it travel...10 miles, 15 miles, etc., and how long did I see it while I was watching it depart...5 seconds, 10 seconds etc. The *slowest* number I came up with was like 1800 MPH...and there was no sound. Dead silence.

And the turn...if it was a 747 and it banked right 45 degrees at that distance from me it would have fallen out of the sky. If it were 3 smaller craft like fighter jets further away...it could complete the maneuver, but the engines would be screaming, and they could still not depart the area to the south at that speed, just not possible.

There is no doubt in my mind that this was not a vehicle from this planet, military or otherwise...it just can't be...

Jim, Howells, NY, 1995

Jim was in his twenties and living at his mother's house in Howells, New York in 1995. He went to take the garbage out one night, so he turned on the front porch light. This was no ordinary light, as his mother had installed an extremely bright spotlight that did not aim down, it aimed straight ahead, so the angle of its beam went up into the sky, as well. Without that powerful beam of light, Jim never would have seen what passed overhead.

"It was like something out of *Battlestar Galactica*! It was an enormous metallic triangle and I could see a lot of detail."

The craft did not have any lights on, but as it was only at an altitude of a couple of hundred feet, the spotlight illuminated the underside.

"It wasn't moving really fast, but it was going along at a good clip. Even so, it took many seconds to pass completely overhead."

I asked Jim what he would compare the size to, a house, a plane, a football field?

"At least three football fields," he replied without hesitation.

As he began by making a science fiction spaceship comparison, I mentioned the opening scene of *Star Wars* where the Imperial Star Destroyer just keeps coming and coming across the screen.

"I never thought of that, but that's what it was like. It was just enormous."

"Any sound?" I asked.

"Absolutely silent," he stated. "Had that spotlight not been on, I don't think I would have even noticed it."

Jim then drew a sketch of where his mother's house was and the direction the craft was traveling. After consulting Google maps when I got home, I was able to determine that the huge, silent, triangle had been traveling roughly from the northeast to the southwest. Depending on the angle, it would have been heading from the Pine Bush/Shawangunk Mountain area, toward the High Point State Park area in New Jersey.

I asked what his immediate reaction had been to the sighting, and how it made him feel. In the spirit of a picture being worth a thousand words, rather than trying to describe it, he struck a pose and expression of extreme surprise and amazement. That said it all.

Finally, I asked if he had any other sightings, or had any other family members ever seen anything. Jim said that was his one and only sighting, but he thought a moment before answering the second half of my question. In that brief moment, I thought to myself, *Here it comes, another multigenerational sighting!* Sure enough, he responded with the following.

"Well, my mother and her parents had a sighting when they were driving, somewhere back in the 1960s. I remember my grandfather telling me the story. And my grandmother and mother all backed up that story."

I asked if his mother was still alive and would be willing to speak to me, but he was able to do one better—his grandmother was still alive and would be happy to speak with me. The next morning, I called Dorothy Wiik in Goshen and she was kind enough to share her recollections of the event. Her story is in the next chapter.

Walkill, NY, April 2012

I would like to thank C. Burns (www.pinebushanomaly.com) for conducting and recording this interview, and sharing it with me.

"Brad" is a police officer who served in the military. He has seen a lot over the years, but few things to compare to what he saw one night in mid-April of 2012. He had to bring his wife to the hospital in Newburgh, and as he and his 16-year-old daughter were driving home to Walkill, they saw something odd.

It was about 10pm, and as they approached the intersection of Routes 32 and 300, they noticed a very bright white light in the sky, about a mile away, that appeared stationary. With their proximity to Stewart Airport, Brad's initial thought was that a jet was coming toward them for a landing, which is why it didn't appear to have any side to side or up and down motion. Watching it for a few minutes, however, the object didn't move at all, so they ruled out a jet or airplane. It appeared as though the object was hovering in the area of the large electrical tower on the hill in Plattekill.

Then a beam of light came out of it, pointing straight down to the ground, and Brad then concluded it must be a helicopter. In describing the beam of light, Brad compared it to an incandescent bulb with a yellowish or golden cast to it, which admittedly he thought was odd for a helicopter. After about five minutes of watching this craft with the bright beam, it simply disappeared. Of course, it could have simply been a helicopter that turned off its lights, but what happened next made the helicopter theory impossible.

The craft suddenly reappeared "many miles to the west," and "helicopters don't go that fast," Brad realized. He described his interest in aircraft when he was in the military, and said that "any aircraft they let us see didn't move like that." Could our military have secret aircraft that can hover *and* travel and tremendous speeds? Possibly, but it got even stranger.

When they got home, they continued to observe the object, "which almost looked like a comet the way it was going across the sky." With open fields stretching out for a couple of hundred yards, and only a few other houses in the area, they had a clear view of the object in the clear, dark skies. To get an even better view, Brad got his digital camera to zoom in and try to make out more detail.

"I wish the camera had a card in it," Brad lamented. "Actually, it did have a card, but it was full of my wife's pictures and videos, and I'm more afraid of her than anything I saw!"

So, even though we was unable to take a picture of the object at that point, he could see that it was not a single craft—there were other smaller ones next to it.

"What it basically was, was this bright thing that had beams of light coming out of it. That was the main thing we were seeing. Really, it had no shape or form, just a bright light with other beams coming out of it. But then, in a triangular form, there were three other lights and this golden object was, I guess you would say, more to the right corner of it. They were off to the side, almost like they were an escort of it. Then on the right corner there were two lights and they were really unique. They were very bright, rotating with all different colors, and they were in a perfect pattern.

"They all traveled moving horizontally, and they slowly moved out into the distance. It was almost like they were searching for something."

Brad went on to describe again how bright the main object was, and that the other objects were "not visible to the naked eye." As they were able to watch this craft from their home for about 15 minutes, he did use his daughter's video camera to film the lights, but the quality was too poor to make out any details. Brad even had time to call his friend nearby to see if he was also watching the strange light, but his friend had taken a sleeping pill and was "an Ambien zombie," so was of no help.

However, in the days following, Brad did post his sighting on Facebook, and several people responded that they had also seen the bright object that night. As C. Burns pointed out, "multiple eyewitness reports" are "astronomically more important than single person sightings."

Speaking of multiple eyewitnesses, Brad then went on to say that in the 1980s when he was a teenager living in Ossining, "a group of people" in the neighborhood called to say they were watching a UFO. Brad was with ten other people who went outside and witnessed a large, bright light "with other lights moving in and out of it." This sighting was very intense, as the lights were "no more than 1,000 feet directly overhead." Brad said that this sighting caused him "to always look up after that." That experience, along with his years in the military and his career as a police officer make him "tend to observe things."

MUFON Reported Sighting, Middletown, NY, May 24, 2012, 1:15am

Driving home from work on Route 84 Westbound. Past exit 5 and heading towards exit 4. Approx 13 mile stretch of country. Started seeing 3 extremely bright white lights in sky. Thought it was a plane heading into nearby Stewart Airport for a landing. Been traveling this same stretch of road for 9 years now at this time of night and am familiar with the airplanes at night. But this wasn't acting like an ordinary airplane. It struck me odd, it was fairly low and appeared to be hovering. It looked so odd.

I was driving 65 MPH and kept getting closer to the bright lights. Then I did see some faint red lights and reassured myself that it had to be a plane. Kept driving closer to it until I passed right by it. It was on my right, just on the other side of the eastbound lanes. It was not moving. It was indeed hovering. Difficult to drive, because I just kept looking at it, so I slowed down.

It was just hanging there. A triangle shape with 3 very bright lights at the corners and a little red light near each big white light. Don't think it was huge as it seemed really close, hovering just above the tree line. Never saw any kind of craft just hover in one place in the sky. Became afraid and drove very fast home.

Trish, Warwick, NY, 2013

There's nothing like having a UFO sighting directly over the building where I just gave a UFO lecture, but let me back up a few months.

Trish and her husband live in Warwick in the more sparsely populated area west of town, between Route 94 and Pine Island Turnpike. On numerous occasions throughout the summer of 2013, they saw strange aircraft overhead near their home. Trish described the craft as being roughly triangular, and shaped "like angel wings along a center body." These "wings" had yellowish-white lights and the body was "charcoal black."

There was never any sound, and these craft hovered "quite a bit above the trees," but "much lower than aircraft." They were not very big— maybe just "big enough for two people." They appeared at all different times of night, but never very late. They would hover "99% of the time" and then take off.

Trish believes these craft are U.S. military drones, while her husband thinks they are extraterrestrial craft.

They had a closer sighting in September while they were at the Warwick Drive In. They were watching *Ironman 3*, and not enjoying it very much, so their eyes were not always fixed on the screen. At one point, a light over by the Price Chopper supermarket across the street caught their attention. It was another one of those triangular craft, and this time it was much lower, and it was beaming a bright, white light down onto Route 94. Once again, the craft was silent, and clearly not any conventional aircraft.

Which brings us to October 17, and my UFO lecture at the Wisner Library in Warwick. Trish and her husband attended the lecture, and when I was finished, she gave me her phone number and said she had a story to share. When I called her a day or two later, she gave me all the information about the sightings during the summer and at the drive in, and then she kind of shocked me. It seems that as they left my lecture and went into the parking lot, a triangular craft was over the library!

Unfortunately, it wasn't there long enough for them to go back inside and get me, but while I missed it, I am nonetheless intrigued by the possible implications. Was this a coincidence that a UFO was hovering above my UFO lecture? Was it a government drone and someone with a sense of humor was trying to freak out people who had just attended the lecture? Or, was it truly a craft from some other world, taking the opportunity to make a little demonstration to those who believe in ETs?

I don't know, but I am certainly going to start looking up after all my future UFO lectures!

Last Minute Addition: **Joan Naylor, Yorktown Heights, c.1980, Gardiner, NY, 2009**

Our UFO sighting happened in the late 70s or early 80s when we lived in Yorktown Heights, Westchester County. We were taking a ride one night on rt.129 around the Croton Reservoir. It was a moonless night so the stars were very bright. One star caught my attention because of the orange color. I was watching this star when I noticed that it seemed to be moving. I told my husband what I saw, and he said he had also been watching the same star.

We watched it streak across the sky trailing what looked like fire; our first thought was it was a comet or a plane on fire. We pulled off the road and got out of the car. We saw a large bright light and realized that it was lighting up the sky around it and we could see blue sky and clouds. Suddenly, a very intense light came on, and the object changed direction, coming right towards us. It passed right over our car, about 300 feet above us, and went over the reservoir —it was silent, triangle shaped with white lights on each point, and 200-300 feet long per side. We drove to the top of the Croton Dam to see if we could see it again, and parked on the other side. My husband got out of the car, and we then noticed a bright light on the top of the mountain on the opposite side of the dam.

The light started to rise when we heard a loud roar. Looking over the dam towards Croton, we saw 3 spot lights heading right for us from the valley below. These three lights and the one on the mountain turned out to be military helicopters. The one on the mountain and the three coming over the dam joined up and went out over the reservoir. I watched the local paper for reports of this UFO. A week later, it was reported that someone else had seen the craft when it entered the atmosphere. I called the local paper and police, but no one was interested.

Our last UFO experience happened in Oct. of 2009. We were on Albany Post Road (in Gardiner) on our way to Albany Airport. It was about 2am. We were maybe 4 miles south from the intersection of Rt.44/55 when a bright light came on over our car, lighting up the whole interior. I couldn't see anything because it was directly over the car, but I knew there were no homes or phone poles with lights in the area. The light stayed on for maybe 10 seconds before going out. After going out, there was a flash of light over the mountains on the horizon, going from the center and flashing out over the horizon lighting up the mountains.

3
Disks, Ovals, and Circular Craft

Dorothy Wiik, Chester, NY, c. 1968

Dorothy, her husband, and teenage daughter were driving along Route 17 in Chester when they spotted a circle of red lights in the sky. It was a huge, circular craft, and it was moving back and forth across the highway. Mr. Wiik pulled over and stopped the car to watch it.

The craft wasn't low enough to see any details of its surface, but other than the red lights, there was something that stood out—a bright "light beam came down" from it. The beam didn't pass directly over their car, but it did illuminate the ground as it moved back and forth. Then the craft just took off suddenly at a high rate of speed and was gone. It didn't make any sound when it accelerated, or at any other point during the sighting.

They reported the sighting to the police, and found out that many other people had called, as well. They also found out that many police officers had seen this same circular craft. The local newspaper, the *Times Herald Record*, had an article about all the sightings, mentioning how many policemen had witnessed the UFO.

Apparently, someone in government was paying attention to these sightings, as a man from Stewart Air Force Base came to the Wiik's house to question them. Dorothy said he was very polite, until they told him about the large circular craft.

"He just scoffed at it," Dorothy said, "but then acted in a professional manner again."

Diana Eschmann
Hollywood, Florida, 1973 and Warwick, NY, 2012, 2013

It was the summer of 1973, and Diana and her family were visiting her husband's aunt in Hollywood, Florida. It was almost time for dinner when Diana's kids came running in the house shouting that everyone had to come outside and look at the thing in the sky.

Humoring the kids, they went outside, expecting that whatever it was would be more imagination than substance. On the contrary, however, what they saw was monumental and life-changing.

"It was a HUGE flying saucer," Diana told me when I interviewed her over the phone in November of 2013. "It was at least the size of a football field and it was so low, just at the top of the trees, less than 100 feet in the air."

The craft was silently hovering over some houses at the end of the block, and everyone in the neighborhood was out in the street watching it.

"It was not really black, more of a dark gun metal color. I couldn't see any windows, and at first there were no lights. It was round, with a slight dome-shape on the bottom. The best way I could describe the top was that it was shaped like an old-fashioned bowler hat."

When I asked how she and the other people reacted, I was surprised to hear that many of the residents were somewhat blasé, as they said, "We see things all the time around here," although, no one seemed willing to stand directly under it. As a visitor, Diana was not so nonchalant about the enormous saucer-shaped craft.

"I was so nervous! I knew it was a UFO. I kept going back in the house because I was scared. I didn't know what to do, I felt like a caged animal."

Other residents must have also been frightened, as several called the police. After about 15 minutes, someone on the street reported that the police were saying that there was nothing to worry about because it was just Cape Canaveral was "testing a new machine." I checked Google Maps and found that Hollywood was 187 miles from Cape Canaveral. It seems unlikely that NASA or the Air Force would test an experimental vehicle over a residential area a couple of hundred miles from the cape, but I guess the cops needed an excuse to keep people from panicking.

And then it got even stranger and more frightening. As dusk approached, a band of different colored bright lights lit up around the middle of the craft.

"It looked like that band of lights was spinning, but I don't think it was actually moving. I think it was the way the lights were flashing that only made it look like they were moving."

The tense silence of the scene was then broken by a loud sound.

"At least eight military helicopters approached it and completely surrounded this thing. I thought, *Oh my God! Something is going to happen!* I was so nervous I stood in the doorway to the house. The helicopters were so low I could see the pilots. And all the helicopters were facing the saucer; it was like a standoff. When it got dark, the helicopters all turned their lights on it. About ten minutes later it started to slowly float away, with the helicopters still surrounding it. It finally floated out of sight."

The entire incident lasted at least half an hour, although "it seemed like forever" to Diana. The memory of the night is still vivid, even 40 years later. Over those decades, she has watched TV shows on all types of innovative and experimental aircraft, but she "never saw anything like what" she saw that night.

She rarely spoke about the incident, but when she did she got the usual skepticism and ribbing from family and friends.

"My brothers and sisters said I was weird, even though I told them it wasn't just me. A lot of people saw it."

As I have often heard from UFO witnesses, it is stressful to carry these experiences with them throughout their lives, afraid of ridicule if they ever told their stories. Fortunately for Diana, one day she attended one of the United Friends Observers meetings in Pine Bush.

"What a relief to be able to tell my story, and to be in a room full of people who understood. I felt so much better!"

I then asked if she had ever any other sightings, and she replied that in the fall of 2012, she and her husband were returning to their home in Warwick about 11:30pm on a Friday night.

"The sky was clear and the stars were beautiful, so I suggested we get a blanket and sit outside for a while. I saw a plane, and behind it was a bright light. As I wondering what it was, the light shot across the sky."

Diana was shocked at the speed of the light, and the fact that it moved in a straight line across the sky until it was out of sight.

"I've seen a lot of shooting stars, and this was no shooting star!"

The following week, she attended one of the Pine Bush meetings, and when it came time to share sightings, Diana mentioned the bright light.

"One of the men there asked me if this had happened last Friday night in Warwick. I was really surprised! He said a friend had called him and said she was in Warwick that night and described seeing the same thing."

A more recent sighting took place during the summer of 2013 (when there was a mini wave of sightings in Warwick). As Diana and her husband were headed into the downtown area one night, they spotted a strange, stationary light. They ran some errands, and on the way back home they noticed the light was still in the same spot. It wasn't a star or planet, as it was so low in the sky, so she suggested they try to get closer to it to see what it could be.

It appeared to be over the Hickory Hill Golf Course off Route 17A, so they turned into the road that went through the golf course.

"As we got to the top of the hill the light took off fast! It had been in that area for hours but when we got close it shot off. It was like it knew we were looking at it."

Central Valley, NY, March, 1982

It was a Sunday evening, somewhere after 7pm, as "60 Minutes" had just started. Joe was sitting in his living room watching the show in his third-floor, Central Valley apartment on Route 32. It was late March, and while the calendar may have indicated it was spring, there was a light snow/rain mix falling, but the snow was not sticking to the ground.

The shade on the window was pulled down about three-quarters of the way, and through that few inch gap, Joe saw what looked to be bright flashes of lighting. While there can be lightning under such weather conditions, it just seemed unusual, and there wasn't any thunder. Going over to the window, which looked directly out to Route 6, Joe raised the shade and was astonished to see a large, orange light "coming out of the mountain," as if it was rising right out of the ground.

Having the presence of mind to grab his camera, he took several pictures. Then as he stared at this strange orange light trying to figure out what it was, he noticed what he thought was a star behind it. Joe recalls thinking it was odd that even with the precipitation there was a star visible. Then that "star" did something remarkable.

The white light raced forward so quickly in his direction that Joe responded in a defensive way as if he was about to be hit.

"I dropped to my knees and ducked!" Joe explained, instinctively reacting to what appeared to be an object on a rapid collision course with his building.

When he stood up again, he saw that the object was hovering over the mountain less than a mile from the orange light, and it was certainly no star.

"It was circular in the front, disk-shaped, but thick. And there was a row of rectangular windows around the rim in the middle. I remember the number seven for some reason, so maybe I counted seven windows. The light from those windows was lighting up the whole thing, and it was made of a silvery, metallic metal."

I had hoped that Joe also had the presence of mind to photograph this craft, but unfortunately the sight of this disk provoked an entirely different response.

"I couldn't move. It was like I was hypnotized staring at this thing, and I couldn't tell you if I watched if for one minute or half an hour. I had a 35mm camera around my neck and I never even thought about using it."

Despite his paralysis, he did notice its size in relation to the cars moving along Route 6.

"This thing was huge, at least 50 to 60 car lengths in diameter. And the windows were each about two to three car lengths wide. I could hear the cars going by on Route 6, but this thing was absolutely silent. I don't know how long I watched it hovering, and then it just slowly descended behind the mountain.

"As soon as it was out of sight I was able to move again. I immediately ran all around the building asking everyone if they saw it. Then I went back to the window and within half an hour there were three helicopters with searchlights going over the area where I first saw the orange light. I felt like yelling at them, 'No, not there! Search a mile up the road where the craft was!'

"They searched for a while, but suddenly I lost interest and went back to watching television. It was the weirdest thing—here was the most incredible thing I ever saw in my life, and it was like I didn't care."

The next day he told his friend, and they took a ride up Route 6, but there wasn't anything to be found. His friend, who was more interested in the experience than Joe, also bought all the local newspapers, but there wasn't a word about the orange light, the craft, or the search helicopters.

The view of the mountains heading east on Route 6.
(Two photos were connected to provide a better view.)

To this day, Joe can't understand his complete lack of interest after his spectacular sighting. He also still can't explain some other odd behavior.

"From that night, I never slept in my bedroom again. I had lived there three years with no problems, but that night I started sleeping on the couch. I had a really nice bed, too, but for some reason it was like I was afraid to go in the bedroom, which doesn't make sense, because I watched the whole thing from the living room window."

Months passed, yet still Joe slept on the couch every night. Then the following February, he awoke and "the apartment was pitch black." He heard a noise in the bedroom and felt as if something "blacker than black" came at him. Terrified by the experience, he left the apartment in the middle of the night and never went back. When I asked if he could show me where this apartment was located, he agreed, but said he wouldn't even go into the parking lot—that's how afraid he is over thirty years later!

We then discussed at length his thoughts and feelings about the experiences, and their lasting effects. Even though he's lived in other places for the last three decades, he still needs to sleep with the radio on, or a fan, or "anything that makes noise." Yet he said that he never connected his fear of the bedroom with his UFO sighting, or the thing that was "blacker than black." That seems to be remarkable, but I have repeatedly found that witnesses often have "disconnects" about their experiences.

I asked if his fear might stem from the experience being more than just a sighting, perhaps something involving closer contact.

"Oh, I hope not!" he replied quickly and with considerable emotion, then continued in a more subdued tone. "I've wondered. I've wondered…"

As to his immediate disinterest and lack of caring about his sighting, those feelings lasted about 18 years, and then left as suddenly as they came. Beginning about the year 2000, Joe started thinking about the orange light and the craft all the time. In fact, he still regularly goes over to the Target store parking lot, which has an ideal view of the mountain, and just sits and stares for long periods of time.

On a positive note, several months after his sighting in 1982, Joe initiated some major life-altering changes, which have benefitted him ever since. Whether or not his decision to change was influenced by what he saw remains an open question.

As to the sighting itself, Joe believes that the orange light was some sort of beacon for the large craft to follow. Where the craft eventually descended was near the lake at the bottom of the hill on Route 6 as you're heading east. He knows that area is where the property line of West Point begins, but doesn't know how that might be related, or if the helicopters were from the Army.

What are we to make of all of this? Of course, some people will say Joe was dreaming or hallucinating about the orange light and the disk-shaped metallic craft. But do three helicopters go searching for hallucinations? And what about him ducking and dropping to his knees because the craft was making a beeline for his building, yet when he stood up and looked, the craft was hovering about a mile away? And how could Joe be unable to tell if "one minute or half an hour" had passed?

Then there was the fear of his bedroom, and the strange disinterest, which just as strangely returned to fascination after almost two decades. And the "darker than dark" entity which caused him to move out in the middle of the night is certainly another bizarre piece of the puzzle.

I can't say what exactly happened to Joe that snowy March night in 1982, but it does seem to add up to something more than just a sighting. I asked what he expects in the future, and he answered that he is waiting for the day that there is full disclosure about UFOs.

I told him not to hold his breath.

Sally, The Bronx, NY, August, 1982

I didn't consider my possible sighting important at the time, because I saw 2 oval lights shining overhead high in the sky, moving from west to east, but the sky was overcast and I did not see an actual, definable object.

It was a night of the Perseid meteor shower in 1982 and I was on the roof of my 26-story apartment building with my son, helping him to complete a school science assignment to monitor and make record of the number of meteors he observed.

I did not want him on the roof unaccompanied, so I went along with him and we set up our folding chairs. It was cloudy and after staying there for 3/4 of an hour we decided the sky wasn't going to clear and we should go down to our apartment. My son started down with his writing pad and I remained to fold up the chairs and follow him down. It was late, possibly midnight. I looked up for the last time and I saw two oval objects moving across the sky, almost directly overhead and moving in tandem at a slow speed. Their amber light came through the misty cloud cover. They were totally silent, which is why I noted them.

I live in the Bronx, in Co-op City, along the Hutchinson River. Planes and copters are common occurrences in the sky, mostly police copters and planes heading for LaGuardia Airport across Long Island Sound. We are definitely on the approach route. So I am used to flying carriers and they all make noise. But not these ones.

I called a newspaper and spoke to a science reporter for advice, but he said nobody else called about the lights and they were probably planes or copters but were too high for me to hear noise. I knew he was mistaken, but did not know who else to call.

In size, the two lights looked about half the size of the moon when it is full, and about 70 degrees above the horizon. There were no "coat tails" from these lights illuminating anything below them. Just oval lights, not really brilliant, shining through the clouds and moving smoothly along. They took about 10 minutes to traverse the sky.

Charles Santora, Bordentown, New Jersey, 1983

This case is important for a number of reasons, not the least of which is the excellent quality of the report. The main reason, however, is that it illustrates that while we refer to the Hudson Valley sightings of the 1980s, their scope extended into New Jersey and Connecticut.

My sighting took place in 1983 when I was 14 years old, while attending boarding school in Bordentown, NJ. My parents sent me to Divine Word Seminary High School for boys and, as a boarding school, the students were required to stay at school during the week, but were allowed to go home on weekends. At this school we were allowed to go home three weekends a month. So, it was a week night when my friend (who I am still good friends with today) and I were on our way along the walkway that connects the dormitory building to the school building where we were heading to go to study hall. My best guess is that it was probably around 7 pm because it was dark and I'm sure that the optional study hall class was not available any later than this time.

While on the walkway, we stopped to talk and I actually believe, thinking back on it, we were discussing basketball, because while standing there we were staring at the basketball court for quite a while, which was located between us and an inlet to the Delaware River, and about 50 feet from where we were standing. What caught my attention was the extremely bright white light in the night sky that was flickering above the basketball court. It seemed so far away; so far away that I remember commenting that it must be the North Star, which in hind sight was really silly because we were looking in a southwesterly direction.

As we continued to stare at this bright light, we noticed that it was getting larger, and it was slowly on a course heading in our direction. We kept our eyes on it the entire time until it stopped directly over top of where we were standing. I would say it took about 10 minutes for the craft to move from where we noticed it until it made its way to where we were situated and to where it stopped and hovered.

We were dumbstruck as we stared up directly under this craft. If I had to estimate how high above us it hovered, I would say anywhere between 500 to maybe 800 feet. But even 500 feet seems like I'm overestimating

37

the elevation, because to me it would have been lower than almost the combined length of two football fields.

It was not an airplane or a helicopter. I have always been convinced of that, and I was old enough to know that it was neither one of these things. So I looked up at the bottom of this thing and I saw many different colored lights, that to me, looked like spikes of lights shooting out from underneath. I can't remember all of the different colors, but there were many, including red and green and yellow and blue. I remember the craft being almost round, but not quite. It's the shape that I am unsure of, but I think it's because there were so many lights that were spiking from the bottom, which made it difficult to make out the outside contour of the craft.

It stood still above us for about a minute or two before shooting off, and was out of sight in a second as it shot off across the field and over the trees. The speed at which it took off was amazing. It was there and then gone very quickly, at the blink of an eye. Immediately afterward, we were extremely frightened and ran off into the school building to tell anyone that would listen to us. After debating, we felt that it was important to inform the teacher/priest, who was supervising the study hall class that night, of what we had seen.

Unfortunately, he was not interested in what we had to report and I remember him telling us that if we were not staying for study hall, that we should head back to the dorm to get ready for "lights out." Feeling safer there, I stayed for a little while, even though I couldn't study a lick, I just couldn't focus on my homework. After a short time I left and went back to the dorm.

When I stumbled across that video at the link below [he included a link about the Hudson Valley UFOs of the 1980s] a few months back, I was shocked and so excited, because this video, to me, validates what I have always firmly believed, that I saw a UFO, up close and personal. The year and geographical area indicated in this video tell me that the craft that I witnessed could have very well been one of the many Hudson Valley sightings. Although I don't exactly remember the shape of the craft, I am pretty confident that it wasn't boomerang-shaped, I think it was closer to being more circular.

I later received this follow-up email from Charles:

Last week I got together with my friend that I shared my sighting experience with back in 1983. Although there are some very minimal differences in our stories, the main thread is clearly aligned. The differences are the height of the craft and the position of the lights, but what we both agree on and always have, is that we saw something that was, to us, from out of this world.

Matt, Rye, NY, 1984

The following is a compilation of information I received from Matt by email:

I was 12 years old and with my mom around 10 at night out front of Caldors in Rye, New York. The craft was huge and low in the sky where you could throw a rock and hit it. It was something me and my mother will never forget. It was metallic, circular in shape, with different colored lights going around it. There were some symbols underneath the lights— very generic triangles, squares, and circles.

It stopped traffic and was jaw-dropping to the people in the parking lot. We made a call to the police and waited on hold while they transferred us—I'm assuming to the FBI or CIA? They didn't deny we saw a huge object in the sky, but the explanation was that it was seven jumbo jets flying in sequence.

It changed my life and I've stood by my story since I was a kid. I've been ridiculed for many years and never wavered. Thanks to people trying to find the truth, and I hope in time changes will be made.

Theresa Schore, Mahopac, NY, August 1987

My experience was very simple, just a sighting, no abduction (that I remember). I love talking about my experience. It was probably one of the most special moments of my life; it was such a great feeling.

To my dismay, a person I met a few years ago, whose father worked for the CIA, yelled at me that I didn't see a UFO. She said it was created by the American government, as if she knew more than me. She was irate with me and stormed away and never spoke to me again. She didn't let her children contact mine again. It was awful for me and I was very hurt. It made me question what I saw. Perhaps it was a military made machine? But how did they emit that feeling of love that made me feel giddy?

The experience occurred probably in August. It was 1987. I was with 3 high school friends waiting outside a supermarket [the A&P? on Route 6 in the Caldor shopping center] for another friend to get off work at 9 p.m. It was a warm, balmy, clear night with stars visible in the sky. The sky was black dark, but there were lights in the parking lot that were bright and visibility on the ground was good. We were talking and waiting. I felt something above and looked up. It looked like a shadow of a very large oval shaped object. It was the size of a football field, maybe even bigger. There were a few orange lights on the rim going around the whole thing.

There was absolutely no sound. My friends and I started talking about it after I pointed it out. We were goofing around while wondering aloud what it was and how it could stay suspended up there. It was very real, but we did not know what it was. We concluded it was a UFO and were content with the idea. It was the most plausible explanation.

We were not scared at all. We were laughing. We continued talking about other things. Every so often we would look up and it was still there. We remarked about how long it was hovering above us [at an altitude of between 150-200 feet], it was incredible. Bringing it back in my head, I remember feeling really happy the whole time, kind of glad it was there above me. I think it was there for about 30 to 45 minutes. Our friend came out and it was time to go. We looked up and it was gone. I could see only stars above.

We went to another friend's house afterwards.

I was amnestic to this experience until 2004. I had finished reading or quickly going through *Communion* by Whitley Strieber a few weeks before. The book terrified me. I thought it was awful and that is why I quickly scanned it. Something brought me to the book though. The memory of my UFO did not surface until I read an old diary that briefly mentioned the incident a few weeks later, after happily returning that book to the library. Then it all came flooding back.

Strangely, this diary, which I threw out because there were a lot of sad things in it, came back into my hands without my asking for it. My husband just happened to clean up his stuff from his mother's house and some of my stuff was in that old box. It was spared for so long. Even more strange is the fact that a boy from high school had just reconnected with me on the Internet to say hello at this time. He called to talk and I mentioned I had just read the diary from 1987 that mentioned the UFO. He interjected with enthusiasm that he remembered us talking about the UFO when we saw him at the friend's house we went to after picking up our other friend from work. This was all confirmation for me.

To further convince me I was not crazy and it was real, I had a funny experience with someone around 2004. She did story hour at the local library in Pawling, NY. She was explaining to my kids, the only ones there that day, how to do the arts and craft project she had planned. I took the paper plate and said for some reason, "This is what my UFO looked like." I almost regretted letting that slip, but I didn't have time because the lady said, in a demure way also, how *her* UFO looked. She said hers was above her while driving on 684 and it stayed with her the whole time, about half an hour's drive.

Theresa went on to say that she is no longer in contact with the three friends she was with the night they witnessed the huge UFO. She also explained how she felt that the beings in these craft are good, and there's no reason to fear them. She also believes that the truth will come out...someday.

Brian, Pleasantville, NY, 1988

Brian emailed me the following:

In 1988, I was the University Security Coordinator for the three Westchester county campuses of Pace University. In mid-March, I saw an enormous UFO over the Pleasantville campus that hovered there for quite some time. Many people were out on campus watching it, and we were all spellbound. It had rotating colored lights and was not quite round, but not really oval either. After a while it slowly began to rise up further and further, and then just sped off. The next day, the news said the Air Force reported it was their jets flying in formation. There is no chance that is true.

After requesting more details, he sent this follow-up:

I'm going to say it was the size of a football field, maybe a bit larger. It was too high to make out any real details, but low enough to see the form, and that it was a solid mass, rather than a group of smaller crafts. The lights rotated around the outside, and had color, but were dim...not very bright at all. There was no sound that I could detect. I've never seen a ghost or bigfoot or anything of that nature, but I *did* see this. I was so surprised that there wasn't a greater reaction to it in the community.

Dave Benedict, Middletown, NY, July 1988

Dave and his friend, Justin, were picked up from the YMCA in Middletown around 4:30pm by Justin's mom, Joanne. It was a "nice, hot day with a clear, blue sky" that July of 1988. Dave and his friend were twelve, and they had nothing on their minds but enjoying the summer as they began traveling the two miles toward Dave's house on Jackson Avenue.

"About halfway home I felt really weird," Dave recalls.

He didn't know what was happening, but the feeling was intense. He was compelled to look up, and there at an altitude of no more than 300 feet, was a metallic disk. It was about 20-30 feet in diameter, and was "narrow like a Frisbee. It was silver and smooth with no windows, and the sunlight was reflecting off the metal."

"Oh my God! What is that!" Joanne shouted.

They all saw the silvery disk, which kept pace with the car, and they were all in "disbelief" about what they were seeing. They all experienced something else, as well.

"It was like time slowed down," Dave explained. "The whole sighting probably only took five minutes, but it felt like half an hour."

They also felt some sort of telepathic connection with the craft, although there wasn't any specific message or thought they can recall, "just images." What they do remember was that Joanne kept driving slower and slower, and the disk slowed down along with the car to maintain its position with them. Finally, when they got to Jackson Avenue, she stopped the car, and the disk stopped, too. It hovered for what seemed to be only ten seconds, and then it took off with blinding speed, and the strange spell was broken.

When they got to Dave's house, they all expressed how "frightening and intriguing" the experience was, as well as their "intense curiosity" about what they had seen.

"We talked about it for months. We told all of our family and friends, and they could tell we were serious, and they believed us. It was the strangest thing I ever saw, and it was life-changing."

We spoke in greater detail about "the vibe" Dave had sensed, and how he had "felt it before I saw it." While he already had experienced some premonitions throughout his young life, this telepathic connection intensified his psychic abilities and definitely reinforced his spiritual tendencies. Overall, as unnerving as it was as it was happening, he views it as a positive experience, and actually "looks forward to seeing" another one.

Nanuet, NY, March 17, 2006

Over the years, there have been an unusually high number of UFO sightings occurring on the date of March 17, which is St. Patrick's Day. Knowing that a lot of alcohol is consumed that day, is our government scheduling test flights of exotic aircraft, realizing that eyewitness reports will all be considered unreliable? Or, are there clever ETs who are aware of the holiday—and human drinking habits—and therefore decide that March 17 is the perfect day for some low level flights? Or, is it just an odd coincidence?

The following is a NUFORC report from St. Patrick's Day in 2006:

Sighting duration: 20 minutes
Sighting date: March 17, 2006
UFO appearance: oval
Description:

My grandparents were just pulling into the driveway and I went outside to meet them. I was helping them take suitcases out of the trunk when I saw lights far away in the distance moving really slow. I figured it was something I just never saw before and I pointed to it and asked my grandfather (retired army guy), "Grandpa what is that??"; pause..."Well that would be a UFO," completely deadpan. It was low in the sky and was approaching very slowly. Dogs started barking all over the neighborhood. We stayed outside and watched it pass over. It was very large and oval and had multicolor lights around the edges that slowly rotated as it moved forward. It very slowly went off into the distance (I think we watched it for a long time) and I ran inside and called the police (more because I was hoping they would say what it was) and the dispatcher said he was getting tons of calls and he was assuming everyone had a lot to drink this St. Patrick's Day. The next four hours the sky was full of helicopters with searchlights. The newspapers reported the next day it was likely ultralights in formation. I have no idea what it was but you could see the solid bulk of it as darker against the night sky. It made no noise either, and the lights weren't in plane formation. My grandfather read the papers the next day, muttering obscenities to himself the entire time. He was quite annoyed that the there was no reliable explanation.

4
Cigars and Cylinders

Brewster, NY, c. 1975

NUFORC Case
(Note: NUFORC, the National UFO Reporting Center,
does not divulge the names of the people reporting sightings.)

Sometime during an August Sunday afternoon, I spotted an object at the intersection of Rt. 684 and I-84 at Brewster, NY. This occurred in, I believe, 1975. I should add that the sky was perfectly clear. The object in question was in a stationary position above a stand of pine trees at the intersection of the two main traffic arteries. It appeared to be approximately 40-50 yards above the tops of the pines. As I noticed something in the air in close proximity, I thought to myself, "That's just an airplane - Danbury Airport is just up the road."

Turning towards my right (into the curve) I looked up again at the object with a deliberate intent of identifying the aircraft (I have always been fascinated by aircraft - and simply wanted to look at what I thought would be some variant of a Piper Cub). When I actually saw the craft, what I saw resembled a hovering 40-gallon oil drum - but I estimated it to be about the size of a contemporary Cadillac sedan.

It had a series of three rings of blinking lights - the top revolving in one direction - the middle revolving in the opposite direction - the bottom going in the same direction as the top ring. I tried to maintain a visual contact - but at my last gaze - it simply vanished.

You may think this is flight of fancy or mistaken identity, yet the next day, the sighting was FRONT PAGE news on the DANBURY NEWS TIMES newspaper. The article quoted a Danbury police officer who ran home after his shift and retrieved his video recorder shortly after dusk in an effort to videotape the movements of the object. This officer was an acquaintance of mine (since he had married a college acquaintance of mine) - his name is indelibly etched in my memory. I saw the video not long after the incident, and it simply showed a very shaky image of a light.

It seemed much as if you tried to take a video of Sirius with a rather shaky hand. Yet the fact remains that the sighting was confirmed by a credited news organization and a police officer. Anyone can scan the (well the way they did it then) microfiches of the NEWS-TIMES for 9/75 and find the reference, unless the material has been suppressed. I had for years, kept a copy of the paper, but as time has gone by cannot find it at hand. I do know one thing is certain - that what I saw that day was NOT OF THIS EARTH.

Author's Note: One thing I found of interest in this case is the description of the rings of lights. This is reminiscent of Hank Vanderbeck's account of the cigar-shaped object he saw in Saugerties in 1953. It had alternating bands of red and green lights "like hula hoops" spinning around it. (See *In the Night Sky*, page 113.)

Janet, Middletown, NY, 2009 and Washingtonville, NY, 2013

After the screening of the *In the Night Sky* film at the Walden library on April 26, 2013, I spoke with one of the attendees, Janet. She briefly told me about two sightings she had in recent years, and I took her contact information.

On May 7, I gave a UFO lecture at the Thrall Library in Middletown, and someone asked if I ever had any "men in black" type of episodes since I started my research. I relayed the story of the van with the darkened windows at the end of my driveway the day we filmed our first interview last year, as well as the several telephone calls that experienced interference and were dropped as I attempted to interview some witnesses. I emphasized that within the span of a year, the only calls I ever had trouble with involved speaking to UFO witnesses.

Just sixteen hours after making that statement, I tried calling Janet. This first time there was a beeping sound, so I just assumed the line was busy. I tried again, and got a similar sound. Then she tried calling me, and when I picked up there was just static. Finally, she called again and we were able to speak.

The first thing she said was that she had tried unsuccessfully to reach me three times. She later mentioned that in the three years she has had this cell phone and Verizon plan, she has never had a dropped call—then she had several while trying to reach me. As they say on a popular UFO show, "Coincidence? I think not!"

We decided to meet in person to discuss her sightings, and at 2pm I arrived at the Napoli Restaurant in Washingtonville. Over some very good food, Janet relayed the following experiences.

It was a late May of 2009, and Janet was traveling on Schutt Road (which becomes Dolsontown Road) in Middletown. It was early in the morning and she was headed for the Mount St. Carmel Shrine were she often liked to start her day with a walk on the beautiful grounds, and a quiet meditation to prepare her for the day's work ahead. As she approached Randall Airport, she saw something out of the corner of her eye that she assumed was a plane taking off. It actually looked as though it was coming out of the ground, but she thought she must be mistaken. Going a bit further, she finally had a better look at the craft. In fact, it was such a close look that the experience had tremendous "shock value," as Janet described it to me, which lasted for a few months.

There was a silver, cigar-shaped object with windows, and no visible form of propulsion or engine sounds. When I asked how long the craft was, she replied that it was about the length "of that wall to those shelves," referring to part of the interior of the restaurant, which translated to roughly 40 feet. It was about 12 feet thick, but tapered at the ends. It was traveling just above the power lines and was keeping pace with Janet's car—when she slowed down, it also slowed down.

The craft stayed with her at this slow pace for a couple of minutes, and then it hovered off to her left for a while. Despite the fact that she was shaking from the sight of this bizarre object, "curiosity won" and she turned to follow the craft, but "in the blink of an eye it was gone." The entire sighting lasted about five or six minutes.

When she drove to the spot where the craft had been hovering, she discovered that it had been directly over an Orange & Rockland electrical substation on McVeigh Road. As it had followed the power lines and then hovered over a substation, there clearly appeared to be some attraction to electricity.

The experience had such an impact on Janet, she decided to go to the United Friends Observer Society meeting in Pine Bush a few days later. Feeling the need to tell her story, she was relieved to find out that other people had seen something similar in the area, as it "validated" her sighting. These meetings are important to witnesses in the Hudson Valley, where so much UFO activity takes place, as people have somewhere to come together and share their stories, without fear of ridicule.

Google Earth image of the area where Janet saw the silver cigar-shaped craft.

Janet's second sighting was quite recent, in February of 2013. It was also quite close to where I live—in fact, it must have passed almost directly overhead! The sighting began in Chester, just around dusk. Janet was heading north on Route 94, when she saw a triangular object very low in the sky.

"It was larger than a building!" Janet explained. "It had a solid, bright yellow band of lights around the edge, with red in the center."

There was also a rectangular section on the back edge, giving the overall outline of something like an arrowhead:

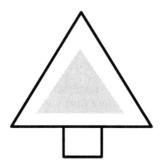

Janet thought that perhaps it was some type of a military drone, but she couldn't hear any sound. She watched this craft moving just above Route 94 all the way up to the intersection of Route 208 in Washingtonville. When she stopped at the light, the object took off so fast it was like it just disappeared!

"I wasn't shocked until that moment. I had been thinking it might be a drone, until it took off like that."

The entire sighting took almost 15 minutes. She would like to know if anyone else saw this triangular, red and yellow object in the area in the last few months. While Janet is certain about what she saw, it would help to find out if there were any other witnesses.

We went on to talk about all sorts of other things, but we naturally kept going back to the subject of UFOs. I told her about my sighting of the V-shaped craft in the 1980s—a sighting that happened to be right by the Napoli restaurant on Route 208.

This area of Orange County, NY is definitely on someone's flight path. Who that "someone" is, is the question!

Between New Paltz and Kingston, March 9, 2013

There was plenty of blue sky on Saturday, March 9, as Rick and his wife Bobbi were driving north on the New York State Thruway, about midway between New Paltz and Kingston. Bobbi was driving, which gave Rick a clear view through the passenger window of something in the sky to the east.

49

"It was silver, oblong or rectangular in shape, and stood out clearly against the blue sky," Rick explained, at first thinking it was just a plane. "Then I realized it wasn't moving, and it didn't have any wings or a tail fin. We couldn't stop because of the traffic, but I watched it for at least a minute or two, and it remained stationary the whole time."

It was difficult to estimate the distance of the object without knowing its size, but Rick got the impression it wasn't more than a mile away, at an elevation of about two miles. He said it was long and thin, with the ratio of the length to the width about four to one, and it was big. I checked the wind speeds for that day in New Paltz and Kingston, and there were 10-15 mph sustained winds, with gusts to 25 mph—not conditions in which any lighter-than-air craft would be able to hover motionless.

Apart from this craft being oriented horizontally, Rick's description reminded me of the stationary silver vertical object filmed and witnessed by many people in the Hudson Valley on October 18, 2012 (see *In the Night Sky*). There definitely appears to be something over our skies which has the ability to stay completely still, regardless of stiff winds. Both the FAA and local air traffic control were notified of the object during the October 18th sighting, and neither agency expressed any interest in it, despite it being in the midst of a very active region for commercial airlines!

5
Rectangles

Middletown, NY, c. May 30, 1985

Rectangles are one of the least common shapes of UFOs, at least here in the Hudson Valley. The following is a NUFORC case, and it is one of the earliest reports of a rare rectangular craft in the area. (Note: OCCC is Orange County Community College.)

Rectangular object, 3 contiguous sections; the outer 2 sections a dark green, the inner a brighter lighter green.

Was around midnight. My boyfriend and I snuck onto the college green at OCCC. No one else was in view. The sky was completely clear; no cloud cover, moderate light pollution. We were watching satellites move across the sky and looking for shooting stars.

He asked me, "What is that?" and pointed up, in a westerly direction I believe. I saw in the sky a small rectangular shape. I'm not sure of the exact size, as it appeared to be pretty high in the sky. If I extended my arm fully, I could easily cover my view of it with my thumb. It was approximately a 4 to 1 length to width ratio in size. It appeared to be in 3 even, connected sections: the outer 2 sections were a darkish green, the center section was a brighter, lighter green. It moved slowly across the sky; it took about 2-3 minutes to move about the length of my hand if my arm were extended, before disappearing. It did not change direction, and moved across the sky with one of the long edges leading as opposed to a narrow end. There was no sound accompanying the movement that I or my boyfriend could discern.

This has always been a very strong memory for me, as I had (and have) never seen anything resembling it, both in terms of real aircraft, as well as fictional UFOs from stories and movies.

Pine Bush, NY, c. Sept. 20, 2004
NUFORC Case

Description: Flying rectangle over Pine Bush, NY late last September? It was late at night last September, and I was at our family's cabin outside of Pine Bush, NY. I stepped outside for some fresh air and to look at the stars as it was a very clear and dark night. After a short while, I noticed a strange flying object appear in my line of sight (a lot of trees on the property), moving in a straight line northeast to southwest. It flew at medium-to-low altitude and at a consistent rate of medium-fast speed, nothing outrageous. But what was strange was that it seemed to be rectangular, with approximately 6-9 dim reddish-amber lights placed at odd positions around the craft (not symmetrical), and it flew entirely silent through the still, cold, autumn night air.

The Orange County Municipal Airport is about 10 miles away, and we see all kinds of private aircraft and ultralight homebuilt planes fly over during the day. But they all make plenty of standard aircraft engine noise, and at night, always have the required symmetrical lighting and flashing strobe light. Though I did witness this in the dark of night, the rectangular craft did not remotely appear to be any kind of conventional aircraft whatsoever. Most importantly, it was totally silent with strange non-regulation lights.

I am a 48-year-old artist, musician, graphic designer, and arts educator from New York City, so I feel like I am visually literate. I am a fairly recent newcomer to this small summertime bungalow co-op here in Pine Bush, though my wife's family has been members for 20+ years. While I have not witnessed any previous UFO activity in the 5 summers I have been coming here, nearly all long-term co-op members have UFO stories of their own to tell from back when this whole area was a UFO hotspot. One woman and her ex- both insist that about 15 years ago they were physically restrained in their beds during a "close encounter" and witnessed a saucer take off out of the neighbor's field. I am only filing this report now as I recently discovered your organization and web site, and just today read someone else's account of a flying rectangle.

Carlos Torres, Pine Bush, NY, January 4, 2013

Carlos Torres' dogs were in the yard the night of January 4th, and because they were barking, he went outside his Pine Bush home to see if he could quiet them down. Carlos works in law enforcement—a job that requires expert powers of observation and attention to details and facts. However, what he observed that night went beyond any facts that seemed to make sense.

"There was something huge in the sky that blocked out all the stars," Carlos recalls, the memory still fresh as I interviewed him in March. "It was a solid rectangle, bigger than the house, and it was moving very slowly and silently. If you put your hands up you couldn't have covered the whole thing. You couldn't have covered it with three hands."

I asked how high the object was, and based on his childhood spent growing up in "the projects" of New York City, he estimated it was at the height of a 20-story building, or roughly an altitude of only 200-250 feet.

His wife and six-year-old daughter also came out to see the mysterious craft, which "was as black as the sky," with white lights near the edges and a red light in the center. While Carlos and his wife were naturally "shocked" by what they were witnessing, their daughter was terrified and was "freaking out."

The large, silent, rectangular-shaped craft moved so slowly that it took at least two minutes to move out of sight. I asked what direction it was heading, and Carlos said it went northwest, directly toward the Shawangunk Mountains. He added that he wished someone else had seen it, too, and through a fortunate set of coincidences, I was able to satisfy his wish.

Before speaking with Carlos, I had sent an email to Ginny D., at whose house we had held our Pine Bush UFO stakeout in October of 2012. I sent her a link to www.UFOgrid.com, which had posted the sketch of the object that Carlos had drawn. It just so happened that at the time, Ginny was visiting her cousin in Florida—the same cousin who had been spending the night of January 4th at Ginny's house, and had witnessed the same rectangular craft moving slowly and silently! (See below.)

Carlos was thrilled to hear that someone else had seen the same thing. Ginny's house is only two miles to the southeast of his as the crow flies—

or as the rectangle flies—so if the craft was headed northwest on a beeline to the mountains, their homes line up in that path.

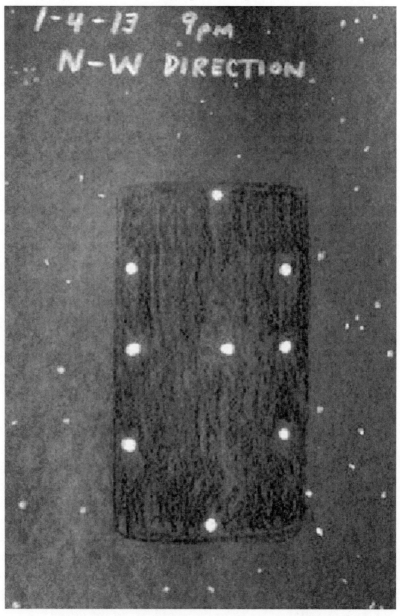

Carlos Torres' sketch of the rectangular craft.

Jeanne, Walden, January 4, 2013

Ginny D's property in Walden overlooks the famed Jewish cemetery and the fields which figured prominently in the Pine Bush sightings of the 1980s and 90s. It was the ideal place to spend the evening skywatching during our October stake out, but unfortunately, the only things in the night sky were planes and stars. However, we apparently had the right location, just the wrong night.

After interviewing Carlos Torres about his January 4, 2013 sighting of the rectangle over Pine Bush, I emailed Ginny to let her know there had been some recent activity, and attached Carlos' sketch. At the time, she was in Florida visiting her cousin, Jeanne. In another one of those amazing coincidences, I got the following response:

Linda!
I am currently sitting with my cousin and telling her the background to the movie, book, and our stakeout. She was visiting us that weekend and took her dog out that evening - she SAW that! She couldn't put it into words until we looked at this article and the drawing! Of course, at the time I was in the house. She came in and told us what she thought she saw, and said "that doesn't look like any plane I've ever seen!" She nervously laughed about it, but I wasn't laughing - because I missed it.

What are the chances!? Ginny's cousin saw the same rectangular craft the night Carlos did, and at the same place where we had held our stakeout. I absolutely had to speak to her, so with Ginny's help, we arranged a phone interview.

On the evening of January 4, 2013, at about 10pm, Jeanne and Ginny's husband went outside with the dogs. It was a clear night, and as she looked up to see the stars, she saw something she couldn't explain.

"What the hell is that?" Jeanne asked, when she saw the massive rectangular object low in the sky. "That doesn't look like any airplane I've ever seen."

They both agreed it was unlike anything either of them had ever seen.

"It was at least a football field in length. It was a long rectangle and it looked like a glass bottom boat. I could see lights inside."

The rectangle made no sound and moved slowly; very slowly. It took "at least five minutes" to pass overhead and move out of sight—and it moved right in the direction of where Carlos and his family saw it. Jeanne found the experience to be "exciting and weird," and was glad to hear that there were other witnesses. She doesn't know what it was that she saw, but as she reiterated, it was unlike anything she had ever seen before, and it certainly wasn't any form of conventional aircraft.

6
Casebook

Ted Winser, Glenmere Lake, Florida, NY, c. 1947 and 1970s

Ted Winser grew up in Sloatsburg, and in 1942 his family began spending summers in a cottage on Glenmere Lake in Florida, New York. He quickly grew to love the lake, the woods, and spending as much time as he could outside enjoying nature. However, when he was about ten years old in 1947 or '48, he witnessed something most unnatural.

It was a beautiful summer night, and Ted was fishing in a canoe with another boy and the boy's father at the south end of the lake, which is very swampy. They were near the west bank, when suddenly, out of the woods on the eastern side of the lake, a bright, round object "like the full moon" lifted up.

"It wasn't floating," Ted explained. "It was moving under power."

The bright object moved through the air and then appeared to land again in another wooded area to the south.

"You didn't see anything! You didn't see anything!" the man immediately began shouting, obviously shaken by the sight.

Ted felt no fear, just fascination. He had never even heard of UFOs before, so he certainly had no expectations or preconceived notions. All he knew was that a big, round, bright craft came up out of the woods, flew through the air, and landed again. He also couldn't have known that this was just the first of many sightings he would have throughout his life.

It was the late 1950s or early '60s, and Ted was with six friends on a hunting trip in the Adirondacks near Paul Smith College. It was a clear October night, and they were crossing a lake in a canoe. They noticed a bright, star-like object in the sky, although it was much larger than a star. Then it started to move.

They all watched in amazement as the object moved quickly in a series of right angle turns, before it shot upward and out of sight. Only Ted and one of his friends later acknowledged what they all saw—the other five men denied the entire incident. Ted was to see a similar object a few years later when he was in the army, stationed at Fort Hood, Texas.

I took this photo from my kayak to show the area of
Glenmere Lake where the UFO was seen.

Ted was later sent to Korea where he served as a medic, stationed
near the DMZ. He had seen several things in the sky that were strange, and
his captain thought he was being "ridiculous," until the captain witnessed
five bright objects coming together and separating again, then heading
north at an extremely high rate of speed.

"I'm not making fun of you anymore," the captain told Ted.

Then two weeks later, Ted received a phone call, and as he put it,
"you don't expect to get a phone call in the middle of Korea." It was a
friend at a radar installation to the south, and he wanted to know if Ted or
any of the other soldiers had seen anything unusual in the skies.
Apparently, they had been picking up things on radar "that were too fast to
be ours," and had flown right over where Ted was stationed. While Ted
never doubted what he saw, it's always nice to get radar confirmation!

The next sighting was back at Glenmere Lake in the 1970s. Ted was working in the area as a surveyor at the time, and he was once again out on the lake in a canoe at night. When he was about in the middle of the lake, he suddenly "heard a whooshing sound, like a glider," and there, not more than 25 feet directly above him, was a circular object about 40-50 feet in diameter, "with lights all around it."

The craft moved to the east side of the lake, where an even larger cigar-shaped object was silently hovering.

"It was at least three or four times bigger than the circular object, and it didn't have any lights."

When the circular craft got close to the cigar-shaped craft, its lights went out and he could no longer see either one. Ted later spoke to a man who saw the exact same objects in Monroe (the next town over to the east) that night.

On another occasion in the 1970s, Ted was out hunting with a friend in the woods on the east side of the lake where the UFOs had been sighted. Suddenly, their beagle hunting dogs—who had been out "hundreds of times"—came running back, clearly "scared to death" of something. Then both Ted and his friend "heard" a beeping sound.

"It wasn't something we heard with our ears, it was like it was in our heads. It felt like it was a warning to stay away."

Ted's friend said, "We've got guns, let's go find out what it is."

"You can go over there," Ted replied, "but I'm not."

He knew if there was something in those woods that didn't want them there, the smart choice would be not to test their luck!

With so many experiences over so many years, and in so many locations around the globe, I had to ask Ted if he has spent his life living in fear, or has he just been fascinated by what he's seen.

"I was never frightened. They've probably been here a long time."

He feels very positive about all of these sightings, and about life in general, but that may be because he confesses to being "a cockeyed optimist."

And what advice does he have to others who want to have a UFO experience?

"You have to be out there. I'm appalled at people who are always watching TV and they don't get out and look around."

59

Despite now being 75 and retired, Ted still gets out quite a lot, volunteering for several historic sites in the Hudson Valley for everything from conducting tours to colonial cooking demonstrations. But he admits he does miss spending time at Glenmere Lake, and misses the beauty, the serenity, and the wildlife.

As to the skeptics, what would the outspoken Ted Winser tell them?

"I know what I saw. If you want to call me a liar, you might be in trouble."

It was a delight speaking with Ted, and this was certainly not a routine interview. My impression fit exactly with what he told me—"what you see is what you get." There was no wild exaggeration or speculation, he simply told it like he saw it.

Finally, I have a particular interest in this case, as I live about ten minutes from Glenmere Lake, and it's where I have gone kayaking at least a hundred times over the last decade. I have kayaked in all seasons on that lake (even once through a layer of ice!), and have often ventured deep into the swampy area—but never after dark. Perhaps it's time I took a little late night UFO cruise…

The Northeastern Blackout
November 9, 1965, Between Middletown and Pine Bush, NY

At a power plant near Niagara Falls at 5:16pm on Tuesday, November 9th, 1965, a surge tripped a relay switch that was set incorrectly, resulting in a massive blackout in Ontario, New York, and six other northeastern states. Over 80 million people were affected, some for over 12 hours. There were countless stories from those who experienced the massive blackout about where they were "when the lights went out," how commuters managed to get home through snarled traffic, and how families had cold dinners by candlelight that night.

There are countless other stories of another nature, as well—stories of strange things in the sky seen right before and directly after the blackout. There were many reports of flying saucers, bright lights in the sky, and a massive fire ball that was seen over the power plant where the surge occurred. Other fireballs, traveling in different directions, were also seen across New York, Pennsylvania, and at least as far as Ohio. Did one of these unidentified objects cause the surge that triggered the blackout, or was it just a coincidence?

The following NUFORC case shows that one of these fireballs was witnessed in the Hudson Valley, over one of its biggest UFO hotspots, Pine Bush.

I am inspired to submit my report after reading two recent reports on NUFORC, one from a man reporting a sighting that he witnessed 37 years ago, and another from a family in Pennsylvania reporting a "fire-ball" shaped object which parallels very similarly to what I observed many years ago in November of 1965.

I had to look up the date of the great northeastern black-out on Wikipedia. I couldn't remember the exact date on which it occurred. On the evening of November 9th just before sundown, I was traveling between Middletown, NY to Pine Bush, NY, to attend the open house in the school where I taught. On the way, I observed to the east an extremely bright blueish-green ball going in an arcing trajectory, passing from one cumulus cloud to another. It left no smoking trail and it was to me the most spectacular and unusual "meteorite" I had ever seen. It was lost from view for a moment while I was driving and as I regained an unobstructed view I was anxious to see where it had made impact. But there was no indication of an impact...which I expected to be quite spectacular! When I arrived at school the power was out and we were all sent home. While I was there, however, I overheard conversations about people seeing a UFO hovering over the railroad station in Middletown. While driving home, I kept my eyes to the sky.

Newburgh-Beacon Bridge, NY, July 3, 1976

On the evening of July 3, 1976, Marloe's family was returning from a birthday party. Marloe was nine years old, and she was in the back seat of the car with her younger brother. Her mother, Cassie, was driving and her father, John, was in the passenger seat. As they were heading eastbound on Route 84, approaching the Newburgh-Beacon Bridge, they saw that cars were pulled over on the bridge and people were getting out and looking up. As there were bicentennial celebrations going on everywhere,

61

they assumed there was some sort of flyover. There was, but it was something far more revolutionary than they ever could have imagined.

In February of 2013, I interviewed Marloe about this sighting, and a couple of weeks later, also separately interviewed her parents. It was a unique opportunity to speak to three family members about an intense experience they shared thirty-seven years earlier.

Marloe recalls her parents shouting, "Get up!" She and her brother sat straight up and looked out the car window. There was a "humongous" craft hovering very close to the bridge. It was shaped like a diamond, but with rounded corners, and was illuminated, but she couldn't see individual lights. She recalls several colors, but mostly a reddish-pink glow. It was "completely silent" and moved in a very odd way from side to side. They all watched this huge craft for several minutes, until "it moved so fast down the river it was just like it had shrunk."

Her father, John, said that he recalls that the enormous craft had an indistinct, "amorphous" top, but the bottom was circular and had windows spaced every few feet. There was a bright yellowish-white light coming out of the windows, but he couldn't make out any details inside the craft.

"It moved in the strangest way," John said. "It just darted away and then would come back. It was like it *jumped* from place to place. And it did all this silently."

As a skeptic, John tried to understand what he was seeing, but this massive, darting object was unlike any aircraft he had ever seen. After watching in awe for several minutes, they were further amazed to see the bizarre craft "shoot off toward what some other people said was a power plant."

Cassie said "it was a crystal clear night, dusk, with no stars" visible yet. As the traffic slowed to a stop, she saw people out of their cars, some taking pictures. Then she saw what everyone was looking at, and it was "the biggest thing I ever saw in my entire life in the sky. It was circular, disk shaped, not a saucer as it had height. If you think of a flying saucer, this was like a cruise ship of flying saucers, the Queen Mary of saucers!" She also remembers that there were windows around the edge, and "some were lit, some were not. There was also a glowing light at the bottom."

I asked if she could tell what the craft was made of, and she said it kind of looked like aluminum, "but not shiny," as the surface didn't appear to reflect the light.

"It would gently tilt one way, then the other, and it was silent. Then it suddenly took off and looked really small before it disappeared."

Cassie said it headed north toward Albany, and she later spoke to people who said it had been spotted further up the river that night, and the police had been inundated with calls. And speaking of the police—when the family got to their home in Hopewell Junction, John called the State Police to report the incident. The officer's response went something like this:

"Yeah, yeah, we've heard. We've gotten a lot of calls. But don't waste your time because it won't be reported and it won't be in the newspapers."

When John asked for an explanation, the officer said that basically those in charge made sure to keep these stories suppressed. He then stunned John by relaying his own sighting. He and his partner were driving one night when "a spaceship" moved along with them directly over their car, and then "took off" at a high rate of speed. They told their superiors, but no reports were ever filed and they were told to just forget about it.

"If *I* couldn't get it in the newspaper," the officer told John, "then *you* certainly won't."

As my research has shown time and again, there's a good chance that if someone has had an intense sighting, there have probably been other sightings in the family, so I wasn't surprised to find out this was not an isolated incident. During the following winter, Marloe was waiting for the school bus early one snowy morning when she heard a strange humming sound. Then out of the clouds came a "whitish egg-shaped" object "with yellow, illuminated windows."

Marloe watched the object until the bus arrived, but she didn't dare say anything to the driver for fear of being ridiculed. However, the bus driver, Jane, immediately asked her, "Did you see anything?" They had both witnessed this egg-shaped craft! (And by the way, Marloe's home overlooked IBM's facility at Hopewell Junction, where several other sightings have taken place over the years.)

Cassie and her sister also had another sighting, and this one was in the early 1970s, just before noon, on a bright, sunny day. They were driving north on the Taconic Parkway in a Volkswagen van, going through a "hilly, mountainous" section, when her sister yelled, "Oh, look up there!" There, in broad daylight, were "three cigar-like objects, tapered at the ends. They were a dull, silvery color, like the other side of aluminum foil. There were no features, no lights."

The three objects stayed in formation as they silently hovered over them, keeping pace. "When we drove faster, they went faster." This went on for quite a while until the three craft sped off together and went out of sight behind a mountain.

Fast forward to 1976, before the July 3 sighting. Cassie was at home and it was a foggy, rainy night. She was looking out toward the woods and saw a glowing orange ball of light descending straight down. It couldn't have been a meteor or natural object, because "it slowed down as it approached the trees" and appeared to gently land in the woods. A few years later, she again saw this mysterious light slowly land in the woods behind her house.

Fast forward again over 30 years to the home where Cassie now lives, in Hilton Head, North Carolina. "It was a clear night, and I saw that same very round, luminous ball of light, only this one was white. It came straight down, and slowed just before it landed," about 100 yards away. As with the other two sightings of the balls of light, she didn't go out to investigate.

I asked Cassie if she had any explanations for what she has witnessed. She doesn't know, but she is certain they weren't planes. When they lived in Hopewell Junction, they saw "those flyboys from Stormville Airport who were flying in formation trying to fool everyone. There was no doubt they were planes, and they didn't fool anyone."

She is also "infuriated" when she tells her stories and people tell her, "You didn't see that."

"Who do they think they are, telling me what I have or haven't seen?" Cassie stated, sharing a sentiment expressed by so many other frustrated witnesses.

Will Cassie, her sister, John, Marloe, or any other family members have any more sightings? It wouldn't surprise me if they did, and it also wouldn't surprise me if any future sightings are also kept out of the newspapers.

For now, Marloe and her parents would just like to find others who were on the bridge that night in 1976—especially those who were taking pictures. There must have been hundreds of other witnesses, and their stories and photos would certainly help document this extraordinary case, and prove that something revolutionary was indeed in the skies during the bicentennial.

LoConti Family, Congers and Rockland Lake, NY
1984, 1994, 2010, 2013

In the UFO field, cases where there are multiple eyewitnesses are obviously more desirable. And when it comes to information, the more details the better. The following is that rare combination of several sightings by members of the same family, and they even went to the trouble to give me compass headings! This case is also of interest in that the sightings occurred in and around Congers, NY—which has had so many sightings that the town had an entire chapter in my last book.

Thanks to Annette LoConti for providing the information which involved her husband, Joe, her son, Michael, and her father, Joseph A. Consoli.

- Congers, Winter 1984: Joe was having a cigarette at the end of our driveway in Congers. He was looking up at the stars, enjoying the evening, when something caught his attention. He was facing Northwest (300 degrees) towards our backyard. It was about 11 pm. It was a very dark starry night with no clouds. Three very bright white lights were flying quickly through the sky in the shape of a perfect triangle. The triangular lights came over his right shoulder from approximately 120 degrees Southeast, stopped dead for about 2 seconds, and then changed direction and shot up in a Northeastern angle into space and disappeared out of sight.
- Congers, January, 1994: Michael, a graduate student at Northeastern University in Boston, wrote the following about his sighting: On the way home from Boy Scouts at Congers Elementary School with my grandfather, Joseph A. Consoli, in January 1994, passing Patricia Avenue and heading North on Old Haverstraw Road, there was a quick flash of green light. Then the UFO streaked across the sky moving South to North towards Trap Rock and Haverstraw and disappeared

over the horizon out of our view. It appeared larger the closer it got to earth. It was moving at an unperceivable speed. We both said to each other, "Did you see that?" My Grandfather went on to say, "Maybe it's going to land on your front lawn on Beacon Street?!" My Grandfather called NASA the next day to report it. They dismissed it as space junk. But we know it was a UFO.

- Rockland Lake State Park, November 21, 2010: Joe and I were both looking to take pictures of the Harvest Moon. We parked facing the lake at 103 degrees Northeast. It was a clear night. It was almost dark. We were the only people in the parking lot. We were backed into a spot facing the lake at the fishing station. There are several mountains across the lake at that point. We saw a round, bright white light rise up from the second of three mountains to our right across the lake. It went up slowly, straight into space and disappeared. We said to each other, "Did you just see that?!" And we said let's get out of here before we get abducted. We checked the internet that night to see if there were any other sightings. We decided not to report it to NASA or any other government agencies, because we didn't want any hassles.

- Congers, 2013: Our final sighting took place recently on a crisp, clear, cloudless night. My husband was walking in our backyard near the driveway at about 9pm. He was facing 31 degrees Northeast. He turned to walk up the driveway at about 125 degrees Southeast and all of a sudden something caught his attention. A solid white sphere, the size of a ping pong ball, travelled in a straight line across the sky going from 60 degrees Northeast to 240 degrees Southwest in front of our house and disappeared. There was no sound.

Annette added the following information:

Joe wants you to know that he was in the Air Force during the Vietnam era. He was stationed at several domestic air bases (Homestead AFB and MacDill AFB), as well as at Da Nang Air Base in Vietnam. He never saw anything unusual at the air bases. He worked on the F-4 Phantom Fighter Jets.

In his lifetime, he has seen shooting stars. He insists these were not shooting stars, because they did not have any tails. Also, none of our sightings had any sound.

He also told me to tell you that we do not drink or use drugs. He will occasionally have a beer, but was stone cold sober each time he (we) saw these sightings.

Also, my dad was in the Air Force. He was stationed primarily in the Southwest. He was part of the Manhattan Project testing. He flew over the atom bomb test sight twice.

I have a cousin who is currently a pilot. He told me that they are told not to report sightings because they will have to submit to psychological testing if they do.

My husband and I are both college graduates and I hold a Masters from Cornell. We are not weirdoes or freaks. We still live on Beacon Street in Congers. And we haven't had any landings yet!

Joe S., Kingston, NY, Summer 1994

I guess you could say that UFOs are like a box of chocolates—you never know what you're going to get. Such was the case when Joe and his sister were returning from seeing *Forrest Gump* in a theater in Kingston, NY, on a warm, summer night in 1994.

As they got out of the car at their parents' house around midnight, Joe's sister said there was "a funny light" in the sky. Joe looked, and the stationary white light was unusually bright, but with absolutely no movement, he was about to tell her it was just a star. Before he could speak, however, the "funny light" started to move, but with a motion unlike anything they had ever seen.

"It started zigzagging," Joe explained, comparing it to the jagged lines used to represent lightning bolts.

"Are you watching this?" his sister asked.

"Yeah, but I don't believe it!" he replied.

They stood and watched in fascination for 3-5 minutes.

"Then we agreed to go inside," Joe said, admitting the sight was a bit unnerving. "And we agreed we weren't going to call anyone to report it, and we weren't going to tell anyone. But ten minutes later, curiosity got the better of me and I went back out."

Joe was surprised to find some of their neighbors standing outside. When Joe asked what they were doing, they replied that a helicopter must have just gone over the house, as a "big, wide, bright searchlight" lit up the area. Joe was skeptical, as he hadn't heard any helicopters, but then he looked up and saw several police helicopters in an obvious search pattern.

"Someone must have called the police to report that object. There were helicopters searching for something, but that bright light was gone."

I searched MUFON and NUFORC for any reports of this incident, but found none for July or August. However, there was a NUFORC case from September 15, 1994, when people in Kingston witnessed a huge triangle with white lights, hovering very low in the sky. People were stopping their cars to get out and look, and just on Delaware Avenue alone, there were at least 20-30 witnesses. There wasn't any newspaper or other media coverage of this widespread sighting.

While Joe could not discern any shape to the object he and his sister saw, this September report does indicate that there was activity in the area during that time period in 1994. In addition, zigzagging craft have been reported in the Hudson Valley over the years, so Joe's sighting fits the profile, so to speak, of activity in the region—activity that still continues to this day.

7

Abduction Alley

Near Spring Valley, NY, 1929

Since I began my research for the first UFO book, *In the Night Sky*, I have developed a particular interest in cases of possible abduction and contact, as well as in pre-Roswell sightings that would be less influenced by alien pop culture. So I was doubly intrigued when I came across a reference to a case from 1929 in Rockland County, NY (where I was born and raised), written by none other than Budd Hopkins, the man who literally wrote the book on abductions, *Missing Time,* in 1981.

Unfortunately, the references were sketchy as to the details of the case, and just because something is repeated 20 times on the Internet doesn't mean it's accurate, so I tracked down the original source— Hopkins' article in the *MUFON Journal*, #156, February, 1981.

It was with mixed emotions that I read the article and found out that this case came to Hopkins while he was being interviewed on WRKL radio (he mistakenly refers to it as WPKL in the article) on November 13, 1979. I was pleased that he had been on the local radio station I grew up listening to (and was actually on several times), but I was dismayed that I missed his interview!

In any event, during the show he received a call from a 61-year-old woman, a retired teacher, who had a "strange, peculiar experience" in 1929, when she was nine years old, in a "small town near Spring Valley," which was just minutes from where I grew up. The details are indeed strange and peculiar, but also eerily similar to other stories people have told me of their experiences.

"Ellen Sutter," as Hopkins named her, was outside playing by a big oak tree on an "overcast summer afternoon" when she saw a blinding flash of light, like sunlight on metal. Looking up, she saw something over the tree, "something huge, shaped like a dirigible, with many, many portholes, and you know, this peculiar light." As she watched, "It was like time stood still," and she felt as though she had become "rooted to the spot." Then several "people" came out of the craft and "floated" in mid-air.

69

She described these people as looking as though they were wearing a "diving suit with a head shape at the top and a very distorted, short-looking body." These floating figures eventually went back inside their craft and took off in the time it would take to "snap your fingers once or twice."

Ellen had "no idea" how long she had watched this bizarre spectacle, but when she went back home, her mother scolded her "for having been gone so long." It obviously hadn't seemed that long to Ellen. She didn't tell her mother what she had seen, because she knew how crazy it seemed, and also because she had the oddest feeling that it was "a secret she should keep."

In the days, weeks, and months that followed, Ellen was "*Very* much afraid" of "it happening again." She was afraid of being alone, and never felt safe. She even developed a seemingly irrational fear of getting sick and having to go to a doctor or hospital. The experience also constantly manifested in her nightmares.

As Budd Hopkins had discovered in all his interviews and research, Ellen's post-sighting experiences were classic symptoms of having been abducted and subjected to some sort of medical testing—frozen in place, missing time, and developing sudden phobias. But even Hopkins admits that the date of 1929 was something of a revelation, as he had previously thought that abductions were strictly "a phenomenon of the post-1947 years."

Having already interviewed a woman who had her first contact in Rockland County in 1937 (see *In the Night Sky*), I wasn't so surprised to read the details of Ellen's case. In fact, where the Hudson Valley is involved, I think I have come to expect such cases, and feel certain there are many more out there, and most likely, even earlier.

What I have also come to expect is the visceral impact of learning the details of these abduction/contactee cases. The stories are unnerving and the implications are very disturbing. One can only imagine what these poor people go through, and the trauma that often lasts a lifetime. Who could be unaffected by Ellen's haunting account of her experience in her own words?

"There wasn't another soul. Not another noise. The birds stopped. Everything stopped. It was like time stood still. Almost as if you were in the present and yet you weren't. I can't describe it. It was like the fields were there, the tree was there, and yet…I felt like my mother was in the house, but she wasn't in the same world I was in…"

Shirley and Pamela, Montgomery and Middletown, NY, c. 1972 and c.1984

During an amazing sighting over their Middletown house in 1984, Shirley's daughter, Pamela, casually told her mother that "they came back to check on me." Shirley thought it was an odd thing to say, but with the excitement of the moment, she didn't ask what Pamela meant by that.

Fast forward almost 30 years to 2012, when Pamela finally told her mother why she said what she did as they stood beneath that massive craft in 1984. It hadn't been Pamela's first experience with something extraterrestrial. In fact, something far more intense had occurred when they lived in Montgomery in 1972.

It was a sunny day and Pamela was playing in her sandbox, which was located close to the kitchen window where Shirley could keep an eye on her daughter. Pamela recalls seeing her mother in the window, and the next thing she knew, she was "on a flat table, like an operating table. I remember it like it was yesterday."

The room she was in was quite large, and there were "metallic pods on the wall." For some reason, she felt that there could have been people inside the containers—but perhaps not human people. Despite the scene and circumstances, however, she wasn't scared, not even when the strange figures approached her.

"They were short, gray, and had big eyes. They weren't talking, but I could hear them speak, like telepathy," she explained. And what these figures said next was even more remarkable.

"We can't keep her," one of them said. "We have to send her back, *she's damaged.*"

The next thing Pamela knew, she was back in her sandbox. She looked up at the kitchen window, and there was her mother in the *exact position* she had been when Pamela was first taken.

"It was like time was standing still," Pamela told me. "Everything was frozen in time and my mother hadn't moved."

Finally, it was like time started again and her mother went about her business as if nothing happened, because as far as she knew, nothing had happened. Her daughter was just playing in her sandbox as she had been just a few moments ago, even though an untold amount of time had actually passed.

"I asked her why she waited 40 years to tell me," Shirley said during her interview. "She said she was afraid I would think she was crazy."

Perhaps Pamela *did* tell her in a way that night in 1984, when she said they had returned to check on her, but she didn't elaborate, and her mother never asked for an explanation. It would have been the perfect opportunity, as no one was in a position to call anyone crazy that night.

Pamela was in her bedroom, and as their property consisted of ten acres "in the middle of nowhere," there weren't any curtains on her window. It was between 8-9pm when she saw lights in the distance, which quickly grew closer. When they were near the house, she could see that it was a solid craft "in a V-shape, and it was *huge*!"

Pamela ran into the living room, where her mother and stepfather were watching television.

"I see a UFO!" she announced.

"I thought she was kidding," Shirley explained. "I told her I wasn't feeling well and I really didn't want to get up, but she was insistent."

"It took me about five minutes to convince them to come and look," Pamela said. "Finally, they did, and then they said they wished they had listened to me five minutes earlier!"

Fortunately, the craft had remained stationary during that time, but slowly, and silently, it started to move—straight for their house, where it stopped again, directly overhead.

"It was so low it just cleared the roof, and it was so large it blotted out the whole sky," Pamela said.

"I grabbed the binoculars and headed outside," Shirley recounted, "but my husband—who didn't believe in anything like this—was shouting at me to stay inside. 'They will suck you up!' he kept yelling over and over."

But despite her husband's frantic protests, Shirley went outside, and so did Pamela. Once they were outside and directly beneath the massive craft, they could both hear a very faint humming sound. The object had "red, white, and green lights at the tips," but the rest of the craft was a deep, featureless black. Even with the binoculars, Shirley couldn't make out any details. After a few minutes, she grew a little apprehensive.

"I kind of hid myself behind a wall," Shirley admitted. But in retrospect, she realized, "Not that that would have made any difference!"

According to both women, this incredible encounter lasted a *full thirty minutes*! They all watched as it slowly "moved off toward Scotchtown."

"Then it stopped, made a U-turn, and came back," Shirley said. This time it hovered close to the house, but not directly over it. It hung motionless over a swampy area for a few minutes, "then it headed toward Montgomery Airport."

The craft began to ascend as it moved off, and then "as quick as a flash" it was so high in the sky that it just looked like an ordinary star. They watched it for quite a while longer, but Shirley was feeling so poorly she finally went to bed. As the show seemed to be over, Pamela and her stepfather also gave up looking.

Shirley and Pamela told their story to family members, who thought "they were a little bonkers." However, Shirley's husband would never speak about it in public.

"He didn't like to stand out," she said. "He didn't know what it was. He would never mention it, and he would deny it if anyone brought it up."

Of course, the fact that he kept shouting at Shirley to not go out because "they" were going to "suck her up," indicates he certainly didn't think it was something from this planet. And perhaps he had an additional reason for not wanting to talk about the subject of ETs and UFOs.

One night sometime after the 1984 sighting over the house, Shirley and her husband suddenly awoke in the middle of the night in a state of confusion.

"My husband was on the floor, facing the other way, so he hadn't just fallen out of bed. I can't recall if I was on the floor, too. But I do remember being on the bed, giving him my hand to try to help him up. It was like he was drugged…like we were both drugged."

This certainly wouldn't be the first instance of abduction being a family affair.

Speaking of abduction, what about Pamela's experience in 1972, when she "heard" them say they had to send her back because she "was damaged." Well, as it turns out, Pamela did have serious health problems when she was a baby—problems that required surgery. If these beings were only looking for perfectly healthy specimens, then Pamela most certainly would have been considered "damaged."

Apart from the vivid memories, Pamela still carries something else from that day she was taken from her sandbox—a circular wound on her thigh that left a scar which is still visible today. No one at the time could explain where she sustained this unusual injury.

Pamela now lives in Florida, where "weird stuff" happens to her all the time, to the point where her "friends refuse to housesit for us when we are away." She has also had many instances of precognition over her life; knowing in advance about things that later happened exactly as she "saw" them.

I asked Shirley if she ever had any other strange things happen, and she said that several remarkable things had occurred over the years—instances of precognition that actually saved her life on two occasions. One night she was driving toward an intersection. She had a green light, but something told her to slow down and not enter the intersection. A few seconds later a car sped through the red light, and would have collided with Shirley's car if she hadn't slowed down. Another time while driving, she also got the feeling she should slow down. An instant later, a tree fell right in front of her. Had she not slowed down just when she did, the tree would have fallen on her car.

This is something I have heard during many interviews—people who have intense encounters or contact, often have a sharpened sixth sense as a result. Whether that is part of the intention of those initiating the contact, or simply a "side effect" of whatever it is being done to these people is open to speculation.

What is certain, however, is that more people in the Hudson Valley than I ever imagined possible, have had incredible experiences spanning many decades. Some carry these dark secrets with them to the grave, while others, like Shirley and Pamela, find the courage to tell their stories.

Brenda, Warwick, NY, c. 1972 and 1977

I met so many amazing people at the 2013 UFO Congress in Arizona and heard so many incredible stories, but one in particular stood out. What were the chances I would meet a woman in Arizona who told me of a

74

remarkable abduction experience in Warwick, NY, just about fifteen minutes from where I live? I jotted down some notes, but made sure to get her contact info so I could get the full story when I returned home. And what a story in turned out to be!

In 1967 at the age of eight, Brenda and her family moved from Yonkers to Warwick, to the Wickham Knolls subdivision, in the vicinity of the Warwick Airport and Wickham Lake. Her father was a NYC Police Officer, and her mother worked for a local newspaper. In 1979, she began attending college at Arizona State University, where she met her future husband, and ended up staying in Arizona, running a business, and raising a family. Those are the basic facts of Brenda's life, but as everyone knows, the devil is in the details—or perhaps the aliens, in this case.

The earliest recollection she has of something unusual happening was when they lived in Yonkers, and her younger sister, with whom she shared a bedroom, started having "nightmares."

"My sister went through a brief time of waking up screaming in the middle of the night, telling my parents that a man was standing at the foot of her bed. I remember waking up to find my parents in the room as my sister was telling them this, but I never woke up while she was screaming, which had alerted my parents to get up and come into our room in the first place. My sister remembers the figure as being a 'little' man."

Of course, every child has bad dreams, but that was just the beginning...

"My sister has a memory of another strange incident that happened when we were about 10-11 years old, during the summer when we were staying with my grandmother in Rehoboth Beach (Maryland). My sister had gone across the street to spend the night at a friend's house, but woke up in the middle of the night and decided to go home. She remembers walking out of the friend's house and out their front door to find the night sky lit up like daylight. She could see my grandmother across the street, standing on her steps looking up at the sky. My sister crossed the street and asked my grandmother what was happening. My grandmother just calmly said everything was going to be alright and lead her into the house, where they both went to bed. She doesn't remember where I was, but she does know I wasn't there in the house at the time."

Although she can't pinpoint when this next event occurred, Brenda also has a memory "of standing in a big room that has windows all around at about my chest height, as a child, and I'm looking out these windows, with my arms on the windowsills, and in awe of all the stars I'm seeing in a black sky. Everything out the windows is just black with tons and tons of stars, and the glass feels very cold, and I'm amazed at all the stars."

Then things got *really* strange.

"Several years later, when we were 13-14 years old and living in Warwick, I believe it was February or March, maybe 1972 or 1973. Our house was a classic Cape Cod style track home. On this night, at approximately 2-4am, my sister and I were in our rooms asleep with the doors open, as it was winter and the rooms stayed warmer with the doors open rather than closed. My parents were in their room, also asleep, with our toy poodle, Bourbon. We were all awakened to Bourbon barking viciously, standing in the hallway just outside my parents' door. As I awoke, I saw that the house was completely lit up with a very bright white light, as if all the lights in a large department store were turned on; a super bright light. I couldn't say from where the source of the light emanated, as it was throughout the entire house. You could feel it everywhere.

"I didn't get up though, I just heard the dog barking and saw my father walk out his door, pick up the dog and walk with her toward the living room. He didn't say anything; he just went down the hall. I don't know how long he was gone, but I remember seeing him walk back by my doorway and back into his room, still carrying the dog, who was no longer barking. Then, my mother called out, telling us to go back to sleep, nothing was wrong, 'it was just a spark that had popped out of the fireplace and burnt the carpet.'

"I just went back to sleep, didn't question anything, and no one spoke about it again for years! The next day my father nailed all the windows in the house shut so that they could only be opened an inch or two. Again, no one questioned him.

"My family never discussed these events, until I asked my sister about them several years ago. She remembers them exactly as I do, but she also remembers that she did get up the night the house was aglow. She stood in her doorway and watched my father walk by toward the living room. She said that our father just stared straight ahead. He didn't turn and look at her, he didn't tell the dog to stop barking (which she did as soon as he picked her up and began walking), she described him as looking like a zombie. She also remembers the nailing of the windows shut."

What was the source of the light, why did her father appear to be in a daze, and what would possess a cop to nail his windows shut? Obviously, a spark from the fireplace would not have lit up the entire house, and certainly wouldn't have warranted nailing closed all the windows! Something extreme must have happened that night, but her parents never explained.

"I have no recollection of any strange event for several years after, until I was 18 years old. I remember the day very clearly because it was Election Day in November 1977 and I was on my way to vote for the first time. I had left my house sometime in the late afternoon to pick up my boyfriend to vote. I remember that I called him before I left to let him know I was on my way. It would be about a 15 minute drive from my house in Wickham Knolls to his house. I left Wickham Knolls and headed down Bellvale Road toward the Village of Warwick. This is a pretty rural area and the road is surrounded by open fields, backed up to wooded areas.

"As I was driving down Bellvale Road I looked out my driver's side window to see a hawk flying along next to the car, looking in the window at me. The hawk's face was right up against the window which seemed odd. I was in awe, he was looking right at me! After about 10-15 seconds of looking at each other, the hawk flew around to the front of the car and was looking in the front windshield at me! I continued to drive forward, so that means he must have been flying backwards, but he was right up at the windshield looking in at me! I was so excited at what was going on, I remember thinking how crazy this was!

"Then the next thing I remember is standing on the side of the road, to the rear of my car. I had apparently pulled off the side of the road, and I am facing the field next to the car, but my head feels heavy and limp at the same time, hanging down, like my neck can't hold it up. I also recall that the ground was wet, and there were worms in the sand and gravel as I looked down.

"I remember the feeling of lifting my head up and looking out into the field. When I looked up I saw a group of figures in the field. They were standing in a V-formation, with a tall thin figure at the point of the V, and smaller figures on either side of him. I don't remember what the tall figure looked like, but he was thin, and I especially remember he had on a tight fitting body suit of some sort and it may have had a turtleneck. I remember thinking that he had a turtleneck on. I can't describe the smaller figures, but they were about half as tall as the middle figure. I remember looking up at them and raising my hand with a feeble little wave to them. I don't remember being afraid or upset, I just waved goodbye to them, and I think they waved back.

"I got back in my car and drove on to my boyfriend's house. I was very excited about seeing this hawk and how it flew looking at me. When I arrived I told him about the hawk, but I didn't tell him or anyone about the figures. He was a bit angry because he had been waiting for me, and wondering what had happened to me because it had been about 45 minutes since I had left to come pick him up.

Brenda's route from her house to Bellvale Road where the incident occurred.

"I told many people about the hawk, and I every time I did, they would laugh about it, telling me that it was impossible for a hawk to fly in that fashion; it couldn't have flown backwards! I agree with them, but that is what I saw. Now, I understand that that was possibly a screen memory, or the hawk was something that I would recognize and not feel threatened by, so that is why these characters appeared in that guise to me."

This certainly wouldn't be the first time that people with missing time and contact experiences think they have seen some sort of an animal like an owl or a reptile. As Brenda explains, the hawk may be a "screen memory"—an erroneous image that masks some deeper, emotional experience that is too intense, so the mind blocks it with a false memory. It also wouldn't be the first time that contactees describe a tall, thin figure accompanied by several smaller ones.

That was the last experience Brenda had before moving to Arizona in 1979, but it was certainly not the end of the story. As mentioned earlier, she met a man at college and they got married and had children. I knew that much from talking to Brenda at the UFO Congress. What I didn't know until I got Brenda's email when I returned, was that her husband also had contact/abduction experiences from the time he was a child. Perhaps I shouldn't have been surprised, as there appears to be some sort of pattern to childhood contactees getting married and then having children, who, in turn, also have encounters.

In any event, here are some of her husband's experiences:

"My husband was born in Burbank, CA and spent the first 10 years of his life in North Hollywood, Reseda, and Santa Monica. When he was about 7 years old, he had an urge to sleep out on the back patio of his family's Reseda home. He lay out on a lounge chair with his blankets and pillows. As he attempted to sleep, he was watching the stars, when a glowing orange ball at a distant point began moving toward him. As it approached him, within 100 feet or so, he became paralyzed. He couldn't move or talk, but he was cognitive of what was going on. He describes this glowing orange object as about the size of a basketball, with what he can only describe as 'toothpick-like points' coming out all around it.

"He remembers it hovering in front of him, but there was nothing he could do to alert anyone. The next thing he remembers is that it was morning! He just fell asleep. Over the next few weeks he continued to sleep on the patio off and on, as if he was drawn to it. He didn't see the object again, but he began having what the doctor called 'night terrors.' He would wake up in the middle of the night screaming and crying, sobbing that a bird was biting his finger. His parents were quite concerned because he would not wake up; it was if he was terrified in his sleep.

"When he was 10 years old, his family moved here to Arizona, where his mother had been born and raised. I mention my husband's experience because the current activity we have seems to be centered around him, and also my youngest daughter, who is 17 years old. She has had many of her own sightings."

Brenda then went on to describe many incidents of "high strangeness" experienced by her entire family. It is clear that she, her husband, and their children are very sensitive to what would be considered the paranormal—only to them it is quite normal! She then discussed some of the most recent events, including what she described as her husband's "first abduction injury."

"He woke up one morning in the second week of October 2009, very early morning to leave for work. He is a truck driver, and his arm, specifically his right shoulder, was aching. He went on to work, only to call me later to say his arm was really hurting, he didn't know what happened to it. Several hours later he called to say he was on his way home, that his arm had gotten so bad that he couldn't lift it. It was swelling, and he was being sent to the doctor by his employer.

"To make a long story short, he had a broken arm, in three places. Two fractures on either side of his upper right arm and a large, round, scoop indentation just below the ball of his upper arm at the shoulder. It appears his arm had been pulled back and above his head hard enough to drive the top of his shoulder bone into the front of his upper arm! The problem is, he went to bed completely healthy, but woke up with this injury! How does one get such a severe injury while they sleep? It took a year for him to heal almost completely, but to this day he still has pain in it."

"A couple of years ago we figured out how the extraterrestrials get in. It was a cold, windy, February night when I was awakened by my husband shivering. His teeth were chattering and he was curled in a ball, shaking. He said he was freezing, so I got up to get another blanket for him. When I put my arm out of the blanket I was shocked to find a cold wind was blowing through the bedroom. It was blowing right from outside the large window against the back wall of our house and into the bedroom. I looked up at the window only to see that the wood blinds and the bamboo shade on the outside of the window had become transparent and the wind was blowing right through them. The window looked wavy, like heat lines on a hot road on a summer day.

"That's when I realized, that is how they get in. They change the molecular structure of the window and they come right through. My husband was shivering on the bed because he had been outside! I just stood there and said to him, 'That's how they get in!'

"Anyway, following the window discovery, High Strangeness took off at new levels. Several weeks later, my husband was preparing for work at around 2-3 am. I was asleep, so he had not turned on any lights in the bedroom. He was in the attached bathroom, and when he came out, he noticed a very dark figure next to a dresser in the corner of the bedroom. He said he felt like a child being scolded, as if he shouldn't be in the room. He turned his head away from the figure and crept out of the room, closing the door.

"You can imagine my shock when I realized he had left me alone in the room with this thing…he said he didn't really have a choice, in his mind he was just told to look away and get out, so he did. He went to work and it never entered his mind again until the next day when he remembered what had happened and then told me. He said he felt powerless, and the whole incident seemed to be erased from his mind for about 24 hours. I have no idea of what happened to me during that time."

It is very interesting about the "transparent" window blinds and the window appearing "wavy, like heat lines." Many people have described floating out of windows or through walls and ceilings. Is it all some common delusion, or have some ETs figured out a way to manipulate matter? It all sounds like something out of *Star Trek*, but that doesn't mean it isn't happening!

Just about a year ago, Brenda and her husband were watching "a program narrated by Morgan Freeman about space and the universe." Her husband began feeling ill and went to bed. Later that night, she awoke to again find her husband "curled up in a ball shivering. He was freezing cold and was bawling his eyes out. When I could finally get him calmed down, he told me about what may have been a dream or another abduction."

"He remembers lying on a table and looking up at a large, flat, round light and he knew there were figures around him, but he doesn't recall what they looked like, as if he doesn't want to remember that part. He said they had a long metal-looking rod of some sort that they had put through his navel and up through his abdominal wall. He said it was very painful, and when they took it out, they laid it on his stomach while they were moving around doing other things. Then he felt someone jerk his head back, as if they were going to do something with his mouth or nose, but he doesn't remember anything else. He feels like he may have been under, but came to, and then went back under again. The next thing he remembers is waking up in our room with this frightening memory; the first time he has actually remembered what goes on when they take him. After this event, he was sick for about a week with terrible abdominal pain. The pain wasn't in his digestive track, but vertically in the muscle itself."

The most recent event occurred to her husband while Brenda was actually attending the UFO Congress. When he got up he didn't feel well, either physically or emotionally.

"I asked him if he had any marks or injuries, other than being sick. He said he didn't think so, but he said his right ankle was extremely itchy, and had been all morning. He then looked at his leg, only to discover a cluster of pin pricks on his calf and ankle."

Brenda concluded her 8-page email with the following:

"Wow, this has been such a long rambling note, I apologize. These are only some of the weird day-to-day things that happen to us. I have too many stories to tell. I am a well-educated, responsible person, not the crazy person I may have just sounded like, but this is our life and these things really happen to us. So you see, I can't just tell you about one situation without explaining how it's connected to another and another and another. I kind of think that is the key to everything that is considered paranormal in this world…it is all connected, and it is all normal."

Vicinity of Mohegan Lake, NY, c. 1980

(While there is no evidence of an abduction in this case, it certainly fits in the "close encounter" category.)

It's not every day that I hear someone describe his grandmother as a Marxist intellectual, but "Don" only used that term to emphasize how she was a woman who didn't believe anything that couldn't be supported with cold, hard facts.

"She was so rooted in intellectual thought," Don explained during our phone interview. "Anything mystical or any type of fantasy was so far from who she was."

And this Marxist intellectual's grandson followed in his grandmother's rational footsteps.

"I don't believe in anything without proof," he stated with conviction.

However, what these two witnessed one night around 1980 when Don was about 12 or 13, would shake the very foundations of what they believed—and more importantly, what they didn't believe up to that point.

Don's grandparents had a house in Mohegan Lake, New York. Every summer, Don and his family would fly up from the Washington, D.C. area where they lived to spend time at the house. One evening, they had arrived at either JFK or LaGuardia Airport, and his grandfather was driving them up to Mohegan Lake. Don's father was in the front passenger seat, and his grandmother was in the back seat next to him.

During the ride, Don turned his head to look out his window, and he was shocked to see a circular craft, about 20 feet in diameter, and not more than 15 feet from the car. The craft was flying at the same speed as the car, and it had "jeweled lights" around the perimeter. The vehicle was also "totally lit up inside," which afforded and excellent view of the pilot.

"It had a long neck and the facial features were human-like, but it wasn't like anything I've ever seen in this world," Don explained.

He described the figure as being seated in front of some sort of control panel, and the skin of this figure was greenish. Don's "jaw dropped" as he stared at this bizarre pilot, who was staring right back at him!

I asked how close he was to this figure, and I got a chill up my spine when he responded, "Eyeball to eyeball."

After a second or two, Don turned toward the front seat to get his father and grandfather's attention, but when he turned back, the craft and its green pilot were gone. He tried to explain what he just saw, but the two men didn't believe a word. Fortunately, though, his grandmother chimed in that she had just seen the same thing. For the rest of her life, she regularly told Don how thankful she was that he had witnessed the alien craft and pilot, too. Both skeptical, rational people became instant believers that there was other life in the universe.

"It's beyond a reasonable doubt," Don stated without hesitation. "They convict people of murder for less!"

However, that doesn't mean he was able to convince his father, who, as to this day, still doesn't believe the story of the saucer and the little green man, even though both his son and mother swore it was the truth. Don's wife is also still in the skeptics camp. Undeterred, Don is "100% certain" about what he and his grandmother witnessed that night on their way to Mohegan Lake. And as I have heard so many times before, he only recently felt compelled to finally tell his story.

While we talked about the obvious suppression of evidence over the years and people's unwillingness to speak out in public for fear of ridicule, Don nonetheless admitted he shares that fear of ridicule, as well as losing his job in Washington, D.C., so he has opted to remain anonymous.

We also discussed possible motives behind all of these craft appearing to people, and Don believes they are simply visits, not any form of invasion. He also never felt any fear during the encounter, "just amazement."

Unfortunately, Don's grandmother has since passed away. I would have loved to interview her, as well. Don also wished he had thought to ask her how the craft left, as he had turned his head toward the front seat. I'm sure this Marxist intellectual-turned-ET-believer would have had quite a story to tell.

Don never had any other sightings before or since, but that one was enough. For him, the question of the existence of extraterrestrial life is truly beyond a reasonable doubt.

New City, NY, early 1980s

Here is yet another case from the "small world" department. Sarah and Felix Olivieri of Big Guy Media and I made some friends while filming *In the Night Sky* in 2012. That included the DiLalla family of Congers—Art, Pat, and their son, Scott, who we interviewed about their sightings. In July of 2013, Scott, who is a film maker in Los Angeles, was visiting his parents for a couple of weeks, and asked us all to come over for lunch. (Which turned to be an amazing feast!)

Naturally, our conversation turned to UFOs, and Art and Pat related a story they heard during dinner at a local restaurant many years ago. They didn't know who the man was (it was a large group of people), but they certainly remembered his account of driving home one night and experiencing a significant amount of missing time.

Scott volunteered to try to track down a name for me, and within 24 hours he had already found out the name of this man's wife. Also, through his contact he discovered that the woman already knew who I was! When Scott emailed me her name, I immediately recognized her from my Facebook page! (Why do I keep getting surprised by these weird "coincidences"?)

A few Facebook messages and emails later, and I had already arranged to interview "John."

It was in the early 1980s, and John was working the 6pm to midnight shift at the Shoprite in New City. After work, he headed home on Route 304 to his parents' house on Old Haverstraw Road in Congers. It was probably about 12:15am when he stopped at the light at the intersection with Goebel Road, which is right by Lake DeForest.

The next thing he knew, he was parked in his spot at his parents' house, over 1.5 miles away, and the sun was coming up! He has absolutely no memory of the almost *six hours* of time that had elapsed. To his recollection, such a thing had never happened before and hasn't happened since.

I asked him if he had any physical marks or symptoms, or any psychological aftereffects, and to each question he responded, "None that I can remember." I also asked if any family members had any experiences, or if he recalled anything strange from his childhood. He thought about it for a moment, and said that he "vaguely" remembered something when he was about three years old. He and his parents and brother "were standing outside, looking at something in the sky," but that's all he could recall.

I then asked what he thinks happened to him that night, and again there was some hesitation, but he finally said that it could have been an episode of "sleepdriving"—essentially sleepwalking, except you are driving a car. While that would be a more rational explanation than jumping to the conclusion of abduction, there are some problems with the sleepdriving theory.

According to sleep researchers, sleepwalking types of activities occur at deeper levels of sleep, which are usually only reached after the person has been asleep at least 20-30 minutes—not instantaneously while stopped at a traffic light. Also, John didn't have any other episodes of sleepwalking before or after, so a single isolated case that lasted long enough to drive all the way home would be remarkable.

Of course, assigning this case to some sort of ET cause requires even more remarkable direct evidence, which doesn't appear to be available. However, there is some very compelling circumstantial evidence.

If you read my first UFO book, *In the Night Sky*, then you know that the Lake DeForest area has been a hotspot of UFO activity since at least the 1950s. Also, and this is a very big also, John's family lived on Old Haverstraw Road—the exact same road where Gary's family lived and had numerous sightings and contact. (Their detailed story is also in the first book.)

I am finding that with UFOs and abductions, it's often like real estate—it's all about location, location, location—and you can't find a better place for missing time and UFO activity than right where John lived. To paraphrase an old saying, if it looks like a duck and walks like a duck, and lives where there's a lot of ducks, then it's probably a duck!

Unfortunately, most of John's family has passed away, but I urged him to speak with remaining relatives to see if any of them have had any experiences or sightings. I would also like to hear from other people who grew up on Old Haverstraw Road or the surrounding area, as I suspect there are many more stories waiting to be told.

Gayle, Pomona, NY, August 25, 1984

Gayle attended one of my UFO lectures in 2013, which "brought back memories" of her own experience, which is related in the following:

As I remember it was late summer, I believe Saturday night, August 25th, 1984. Me and my boyfriend were walking down the dirt road in Pomona Country Club heading towards my house, which was on a dead end street that backed up to the woods. We had my dog with us and we noticed a light glowing in the woods. We listened to hear if someone was walking, but all we heard was silence.

My dog began barking and we thought someone was in the woods walking their dog, because of my dog's reaction. We kept calling to them and saying things like ET go home; just joking around. My dog ran into the woods and ran back to us with his tail between his legs!

The light kept moving back into the woods and we realized it couldn't be a person, because they would have answered us and we would have heard something? We started to get a little nervous and walked down my long circular driveway to the front of my house. We saw the light moving farther back into the woods and something made me look up, because I couldn't understand where the light was coming from (it looked like a flashlight someone was holding and walking).

As we looked up, I saw a side view of a huge object, and because it was dark, I could see millions of small lights (can't remember the colors or if they were just white?). At the same time we looked up, the UFO slowly and quietly moved up the hill into the woods. We didn't hear any noise; it just moved slowly away.

We were, of course, shocked, and couldn't believe what we just saw, and felt somewhat scared. It felt like something was looking down at us. When I ran into the house to tell my mother, she didn't believe me until the next morning when the neighbor called and told my mom she wasn't gonna believe what happened the night before. She went on to explain that she was sitting on her back porch, when she looked up and saw this UFO hovering over her yard. This confirmed what I had also seen.

I felt as if they were trying to contact me somehow. Following this episode I did have dreams of beings standing by my bed at night and dreams of them walking down a hallway towards my room. It felt like it was a team of alien beings with a leader. I also wonder, because after this sighting I began getting vertigo and still have it to this day. No doctors can figure out why I have it, even after a brain scan and many maneuvers to correct it.

I also had something happen to me in the 90s, where I woke up one morning with scratches on the back of my neck, and on my arms. No one could figure out how I got those scratches in my sleep?

In conclusion, after I came to see you speak, it brought back memories of this time, and I contacted my old boyfriend, who I hadn't spoken to since the 80s. I found him on Facebook and he confirmed that I did see it, because he was with me when it happened. The first thing he said was, "Yeah, don't you remember the Hudson Valley sightings in the 80s?" So I know I'm not crazy and did really see it.

Jennifer, Nyack and Valley Cottage, NY, 1991

Here's a story from someone who contacted me on Facebook:

You asked about my UFO experience. I remember two. They both were in 1991 in Nyack and Valley Cottage. The first was in Nyack. It was strange—for many nights I was looking out my window, waiting for something. Then one night, I was sleeping on my futon and I was woken up by two beings. I was petrified. I noticed their skin and the way they moved—they had large pores and there was moisture that showed when they moved, and they moved very quickly, kind of like an insect. Then I looked at one of them in the eyes, and just by looking at them I was put out; like I was not able to stay awake. That is all I remembered.

The second time, my boyfriend and I were going to his apartment (in Valley Cottage), which was in a house. We were unpacking groceries from the car, and we saw this space ship above the house, very close. I actually started running toward it, and then it quickly moved and was gone.

My boyfriend at the time never believed me when I told him my experience, but now he saw it, too, and I remember he said, "I'll never doubt you."

Immediately after this happened, a police car went speeding down Lake Road. Sometime later, I saw an article in the *Journal News* about a special that was filmed at Rockland Lake, about a UFO sighting there, so I was thinking maybe that was connected. I actually called the paper to see when this show was filmed, and it was way before I saw this in the sky.

Anyway that's my story. I just wonder why things happen to some, and not others.

That is certainly something we all wonder!

8
Stakeout

Walden/Pine Bush, NY, July 2013

As part of the research for *In the Night Sky*, in November of 2012, we had a "UFO Stakeout" at the home of Ginny D. Her property overlooks the area of the Jewish Cemetery in Pine Bush—the hottest part of the Pine Bush hotspot.

We decided to have another stakeout in July of 2013. In attendance that night was Ginny, my husband, Bob Strong, C. Burns, who hosts the Pine Bush archive of sightings (www.pinebushanomaly.com), and Dr. Art Donohue, our friend, chiropractor, and witness to a fascinating sighting I included in my last book. Considering the bitter cold of the November stakeout, it was wonderful to have a warm July evening to spread out the blankets, set up the lawn chairs, and see what might cross the skies that night.

Bob and I arrived before sunset, which is always a good idea so you can see where the houses, roads, etc. are, to identify possible sources of lights. This is particularly important for Pine Bush, where a lot of the anomalous activity is ground-based. I then watched the air traffic to become familiar with the flight patterns. With Stewart Airport being so close—about 10 miles to the southeast—it was easy to identify the paths of the very low planes that were either taking off or preparing to land there. There was also a roughly north-to-south path that commercial airliners were taking on a regular basis, as well as a northwest-southeast course that a few other planes were traveling.

We were treated to a lovely, colorful sunset, and I found myself taking several pictures of the "pretty clouds." As I was taking one picture, I noticed what looked like a straight line through the clouds, which I assumed was made by some type of jet. But then I noticed in the same frame that there was a circular hole in the clouds, as well. I had no idea what could punch a round hole like that in the cloud layer, but I imagined it had to be something either going straight up or coming straight down.

Bob is looking up at the straight line contrail to the right just above the tree, and the "hole" in the clouds in the center. They appeared much more pronounced than this photo represents.

Everyone else arrived by dusk, and as we were talking, I was using our big 15x70 binoculars to identify anything that moved in the sky. At one point, when it was still light enough to see the clouds and horizon, I spotted a light moving rather quickly to the southwest—several times faster than a commercial airliner, or anything else I had previously seen that night.

"Possibly a satellite or military jet," I announced as I raised the binoculars to my eyes.

When I sighted the object through the powerful binoculars, it was clearly spherical and was most definitely *below the clouds.*

"Not a satellite!" I said excitedly. "It's round, below the clouds, and moving *fast!*"

It was moving so fast, that no one else had a chance to grab one of the other pairs of binoculars to view it up close. I have no idea what it was; all I can say is that it was spherical, bright, and to use the phrase I used that night, it was "hauling ass." It traversed the length of the sky in about 15 to 20 seconds.

There were some other sightings that turned out to be false alarms—lights that at first glance looked suspicious, until viewed through the binoculars and seen to be conventional aircraft. When they got close enough, we could also hear engine sounds. Yet, even without the "Mother Ship" making an appearance, the hours passed pleasantly—good company, great conversations; all while sitting beneath the stars on a nice, warm summer evening.

It was getting close to midnight when Art said he would be leaving, as he had to get up early in the morning. He was standing with Bob to his left, and C. Burns was to Bob's left. I was standing facing the three of them, and Ginny was seated behind them. I was going to kid Art that as soon as he left, that would be when something would happen, but I never got to finish my words.

"You know what's going to happen as soon as you leave, don't you?" I began. "That's when—"

I stopped short because the three of them suddenly lit up brightly for an instant, as if someone had just taking a flash picture behind me. The only trouble was, no one else was with us. My back had been to a section of woods a couple of hundred feet away, and that's where Bob and C. Burns said the flash had originated—*inside the woods.* Normally, that would be an interesting little anomaly that we would take note of, and then mentally file it away.

However, it was a different matter here, because in Pine Bush a lot of the activity is at ground level, and has often been described as a strobe light or flash bulb effect. C. Burns has experienced this on many occasions in Pine Bush, and he had previously tried to describe the effect to me, but I just couldn't quite picture it. I could certainly picture it now!

C. Burns took off running at full speed down the street towards the woods, and after a few moments I took off down the street, as well. We hoped we would see the effect again up close, but unfortunately, it didn't reoccur. We went back to the others and all discussed what had happened.

Could it have been lightning? We could see some lightning way off in the distance just on the horizon, but it appeared to be dull, tiny, reddish, and certainly didn't illuminate anything near us. When I got home, I checked the radar for 11:51pm (the time of the flash) and found that the nearest thunderstorm was south of Yonkers, NY, over 60 miles away.

Bob was certain the light was bright white, and very close. Art also saw the light as white, but assumed it was just "a lightning flash through the trees." He was rather puzzled by our excitement, as he hadn't heard about the Pine Bush flash bulb effect. The next day, I asked for a statement from him to send to C. Burns for his archive.

"I did indeed see a bright flash of a light come from the direction of the trees. I would describe it as what I once saw when I was a teen: A buddy of mine had an M-80, put it in the woods behind a group of trees, lit the fuse, and then came running out of the woods. There was a bright flash and a "BOOM!" This light flash was reminiscent of that light, but without the explosion sound."

So there are the physical descriptions of the flash. Now let me tell you what an adrenalin rush I got from it! I was just buzzing for hours afterward and barely got any sleep. I realize this is very subjective evidence—if it indeed is any evidence at all—but that flash really got me buzzing and made quite an impression, especially because of the timing. I was just in the process of telling Art that he would miss something if he left, and before I could finish saying the words, everything lit up! That's either an amazing validation or one hell of a coincidence.

Also, when I sent Ginny a thank you email the next day, I mentioned that it would be interesting if she took her dog to the field where we were sitting, and into those woods to see if he had any reaction. She replied that her cats had acted very strangely that night after we all left. They had been on the field with us, and every night they *always* followed Ginny back into the house—except this night.

"I couldn't get the cats to come off the field. They followed me half the way back to the house, but that was it...they turned around (!) and headed back to the field."

That had *never* happened before. What would keep the cats from going inside, as they always had done before? What was it about the field that made them want to stay?

I wish some massive triangle or rectangle, bristling with lights, had hovered overheard for 20 minutes so I could fill up memory cards with photos and video, but that didn't happen. Instead, I got a photo of a circular hole in the clouds, saw a fast-moving spherical object, and had my back turned to a bright flash—nothing conclusive, but nonetheless intriguing.

I will most certainly avail myself of Ginny's hospitality again sometime in the future for another stakeout, and I'll have all my cameras, camcorders, and binoculars ready to capture anything in the skies. But from now on, whenever I'm in the Pine Bush area, I will also keep an eye on the ground!

9
Project Blue Book: Stewart Air Force Base

The rash of UFO sightings in 1947 made the military brass uneasy about national security, which led to the United States Air Force initiating Project Sign to study the reports and evidence. Supposedly, some project personnel came to believe that UFOs were indeed extraterrestrial, and said so in a report called the Estimate of the Situation. While this document, if it ever existed, has never been released to the public, it is likely that at the very least, such extraterrestrial conclusions were being expressed internally, which may explain why Project Sign was terminated in 1949.

Project Grudge then took its place, but this was certainly not a project designed to search for the truth. Air Force Captain Edward Ruppelt, who is acknowledged as the man who coined the term "Unidentified Flying Object," worked on Project Grudge, and characterized it in the following way:

"In doing this, standard intelligence procedures would be used. This normally means an *unbiased evaluation* of intelligence data. But it doesn't take a great deal of study of the old UFO files to see that standard intelligence procedures were not being followed by Project Grudge. Everything was being evaluated on the premise that UFOs couldn't exist. No matter what you see or hear, don't believe it."

Project Grudge was then dissolved and Project Blue Book began, running until early 1970. Although the relatively open-minded Ruppelt would work on Blue Book until 1953, the project seemed to inherit Grudge's policy of deny, deny, deny. While studying the PBB case files, it quickly becomes evident that there was a standard list of excuses to be used to cover just about everything short of the mother ship landing on the White House lawn—although I'm sure they would have somehow managed to say it was a new type of weather balloon!

Rather than accurately summarize and judge all the evidence, their process could best be termed as an exercise in "How to Minimize and Misrepresent in 50 Words or Less." It appeared as though whoever was filing the report would look for key words such as "star-like," "meteor," "Moon," or "plane" in the witness descriptions, then try to characterize the sighting into one of these neat and convenient scapegoat categories, regardless of whatever else the witness stated.

As a fictional example, if a witness said, "At first it looked like an ordinary star, but then it started moving and descended as rapidly as a meteor. It was a huge, silvery disk, twice as big as the full moon," the official file card would probably read, "Witness stated it looked like a star. Most likely astronomical event of meteor passing by full moon."

Faced with searching through the thousands of PBB pages to look for cases in the Hudson Valley, I admit I was naïve enough to think that I could get away with only having to read the summaries written on the Project Record Cards, and only delve deeper when warranted. I assumed these cards contained an accurate representation of the eyewitness accounts and evidence. Was I ever wrong!

The first eye-opening example was from Stewart Air Force Base in 1951. (See below.) In a *What the hell!* moment, I suddenly realized that if Project Blue Book personnel at Stewart AFB would mischaracterize, and let's face it, outright lie, about a sighting made by *two of its own officers*, what chance did the general public have of an unbiased evaluation of their sightings?

With the flames of righteous indignation once again ignited within me, I set about a systematic and time-consuming search of *all* Hudson Valley cases, *reading every page*, while endeavoring to be what PBB was not—objective. Obviously, without having personally conducted the interviews, I can't vouch for the veracity and character of any of the witnesses. I only had the case files to go by, and they often only supplied brief or conflicting information.

With what I had available, I had to try to judge who was being honest and actually saw something *unexplainable*, who was being honest but actually saw something *explainable*, those who were caught up in the UFO frenzy and were possibly stretching the truth, and those who were just plain making it up because they were delusional or wanted their five minutes of Project Blue Book fame.

Therefore, I have made some judgment calls, and for the most part, those cases with thin evidence or weak reliability have not been included. However, on the flip side of that, I have included some cases that don't have much in the way of evidence, but the official excuses are so absurd they were too good to pass up!

All this being said, I think what ultimately emerges is an impressive picture of persistent and widespread UFO activity throughout the Hudson Valley during the entire duration of Project Blue Book, as well as the persistent and consistent attempts by PBB staff to minimize, mischaracterize, obfuscate, and conceal the truth.

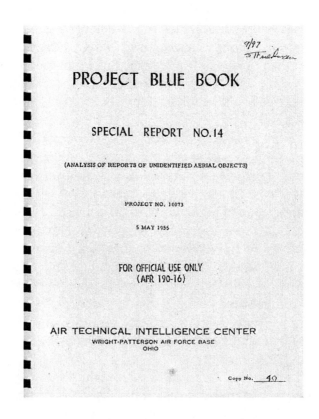

Stewart Air Force Base, January 12, 1951

Another foolish misconception I had as I began researching the Project Blue Book archives, was that I should concentrate only on the "Unknowns," as they would be the cases that would provide the strongest evidence. However, that illusion lasted only long enough for me to read the complete file on a sighting by two Air Force officers at Stewart AFB on January 12, 1951.

To be fair, the beleaguered Air Force personnel assigned to Project Blue Book no doubt had to go through stacks of the flimsiest and most ridiculous reports of alleged UFO sightings, but it's tough to generate any sympathy for them as their primary job was obviously not to report the truth, but to diminish and cloud the truth. But let's not take my word for that, let's examine the following case and you can draw your own conclusions.

PROJECT 10073 RECORD CARD

1. DATE	2. LOCATION	12. to:
12 Jan 1951	Stewart AFB, N.Y.	☐ Was B... ☒ Probably Balloon ☐ Possibly Balloon
3. DATE-TIME GROUP Local GMT 13/0305Z	4. TYPE OF OBSERVATION ☒ Ground-Visual ☐ Ground-Radar ☐ Air-Visual ☐ Air-Intercept Radar	☐ Was Aircraft ☐ Probably Aircraft ☐ Possibly Aircraft
5. PHOTOS ☐ Yes ☒ No	6. SOURCE Two AF Officers	☐ Was Astronomical ☐ Probably Astronomical ☐ Possibly Astronomical
7. LENGTH OF OBSERVATION 2 min	8. NUMBER OF OBJECTS One	9. COURSE Vertical
10. BRIEF SUMMARY OF SIGHTING Shape - Star - Size Star - Color was white to hazy yellow to red- Speed rapid ascension. Alt - Low to high. Ascended in an erratic manner.	11. COMMENTS Evaluated as a balloon.	☐ Other ☐ Insufficient Data for Evaluation ☐ Unknown

ATIC FORM 329 (REV 26 SEP 52)

This record card gives the standard information—the date, time, duration, and location of the sighting, the number of witnesses, a brief description, and the all-important comments and conclusions. First, we should take note that this was a sighting by not one, but two, Air Force officers on an Air Force base. Clearly, these are men who should have training and experience with aircraft, making them very credible witnesses.

Then we read the description of what these two officers saw. It was just a small, star-sized light that ascended, albeit in an erratic fashion. And the conclusion was that it was simply a weather balloon. Odd, isn't it, that two Air Force officers stationed at Stewart didn't know a weather balloon when they saw one?

The next piece in the file was this:

UNCLASSIFIED

HEADQUARTERS
EASTERN AIR DEFENSE FORCE
STEWART AIR FORCE BASE, NEWBURGH, N. Y.

INT 452.1

SUBJECT: Reporting of information on Unconventional Aircraft.

TO: Commanding General
           Air Materiel Command
           Wright-Patterson AFB
           Dayton, Ohio
           ATT: MCIS

       Reference letter, USAF, AFOIC-CC-1, subject as above, dated 8 September 1950, attached are two reports by individuals on sighting of possible unconventional aircraft.

       FOR THE COMMANDING GENERAL:

                                  C J Dillon

2 Incls
  1. Rpt, subj as
    above, Capt Anderson
  2. Rpt, subj as
    above, 2d Lt Gallagher

Info cy to
  CG, ADC, Att: D/I

98

For starters, welcome to the wonderful world of military typos, where documents are "Uncalssified" and reports are dated four months before they happen. (Unless the incident took place in September of 1950 and took 4 months to report.) Mistakes aside, the important thing here is that this alleged weather balloon is being called "unconventional aircraft."

Finally, we have the actual witness statements of Captain Anderson and Lieutenant Gallagher. It's a shame to spoil a good weather balloon story with the facts, but let's see if we can draw our own conclusions.

THIS PAGE IS UNCALSSIFIED

UNCLASSIFIED

SUBJECT: Report of Information on Unconventional Aircraft.

1. One object; unusually bright and a brilliant white; appeared to be three or four times, as large as a star; as object ascended it appeared to change in color to a hazy yellow - green - red and left tail of light behind; no sound; appeared to have tremendous rate of speed, as well as a pattern of flight, although it would zig zag in an abrupt fashion. Observer stated object did not appear to be conventional aircraft and in his judgment displayed convincing traits of planned maneuverability, which discounted theory of its being a balloon.

2. Observation made on 12 January 1951, approximately 2200 EST.

3. Visual sighting on corner of X and D Streets, Stewart Air Force Base, New York. Location of observation point on hill of approximately 100 feet altitude.

4. Observer was 2d Lt. Robert P. Gallagher, AO-1860094, USAF, Headquarters and Headquarters Squadron, Stewart Air Force Base, New York. No previous aerial observer experience.

5. Visibility excellent; ceiling high thin scattered clouds.

6. Observer stated on 11 January 1951 at approximately the same time, he noticed this brilliant object in same general position, but was in sight only several seconds before it descended and was blocked from view.

As you recall, the official report card stated that the object was the size and shape of a star, yet Lt. Gallagher claims that it was "three or four times, as large as a star," it changed color, and it left a "tail of light

99

behind." More importantly, "Observer stated object did not appear to be conventional aircraft, and in his judgment *displayed convincing traits of planned maneuverability, which discounted theory of its being a balloon.*"

I think we can safely assume that what Lt. Gallagher meant by "planned maneuverability" was that, unlike a floating balloon left to the mercy of the winds, this object was being directed by intelligent control. I wonder why this didn't make it into the summary of the report card? Finally, we find out something else of great interest—he saw the same thing the night before, which sticks another pin in the lone weather balloon theory.

Then we have Captain Anderson's statement:

SUBJECT: Report of Information on Unconventional Aircraft.

1. One object.

2. Size undetermined; white light resembling very bright star; round in shape, no tail or exhaust seen; speed was rapid upward vertical motion with an erratic sidewise motion. Upward speed was not constant; faded from sight through very high scattered clouds; no sound.

3. Object sighted 12 January, 2205 EST.

4. Visual sighting.

5. Observer on hill approximately 100 feet elevation first observed object from car. Stopped on corner of X and D Streets Stewart Air Force Base, New York and observed object for approximately 2 minutes from outside of car. Direction of object from point of observation approximately 120°. Distance unknown; altitude from approximately 100 feet above horizon to very high ceiling.

6. Observed by Capt. Robert F. Anderson, AO-1637092, USAF, Headquarters and Headquarters Squadron, Stewart Air Force Base, New York. No aerial observer experience.

7. Visibility excellent; ceiling high thin scattered clouds.

8. No weather balloons released during period of observation; no local aircraft taking off or landing.

This is much of the same information, although Anderson does describe the object as "resembling very bright star" and did not observe a tail. However, the real smoking gun is item number eight.

"8. No weather balloons released during period of observation; no local aircraft taking off or landing."

Game, set, match. There were "no weather balloons released during period of observation," yet still the official report card concludes "Probably balloon," with the comment of "Evaluated as balloon." In addition, there were no known aircraft in the area at the time, either.

So, you tell me how a sighting by two highly trained Air Force officers of an object three or four times larger than a star, moving under intelligent control near an Air Force base, where there are no weather balloons or aircraft in the skies, gets dismissed as a balloon?

Perhaps one could forgive a couple of mischaracterizations within the thousands of pages of Project Blue Book, but it wasn't long before I found myself reading the report card and immediately thinking, "Okay, it states it was *this*, but what is the *truth*?"

The attitude of PBB reminds me of the famous statement by Dr. Edward Condon, whose committee during the 1960s was essentially designed to dismiss the entire UFO field: "It is my inclination right now to recommend that the government get out of this business. My attitude right now is that there's nothing to it. ...but I'm not supposed to reach a conclusion for another year."

There's nothing like choosing the outcome at the start of a project!

So this was my first experience with really studying Project Blue Book reports, and it led to many, many hours of carefully examining cases that occurred in the Hudson Valley. More cases are presented in this chapter specifically mentioning Stewart Air Force Base, and in the following chapter are additional cases throughout the Hudson Valley.

Stewart Air Force Base, April 4, 1954

Official Project Blue Book Conclusion:
All characteristics of balloon sighting are present.
PROBABLY BALLOON

The Facts:
An Air Force Captain and Major were witnesses at different locations on the base:

- Just before midnight, Captain Richman, who was the weather forecaster at the base, saw two rotating white lights approximately the size of aircraft landing lights that were moving up and down and varying in altitude between 1500-2000 feet. The lights moved "back and forth over Stewart" two or three times at a speed of about 50mph. There was no sound, and no exhaust. The objects then moved north and gained altitude to about 10,000 feet before going out of sight. The entire sighting took about 6 minutes.

- Just after midnight, the Major (name blacked out) spotted a single white, rotating light at an altitude of 8000 feet, traveling north to south at about 100mph. It then turned east, stopped, and proceeded to move in an "up and down motion," varying in altitude by about 1000 feet. The object then "departed on a heading of 045 degrees, climbing until it was no longer visible." The Major's sighting lasted 3-4 minutes.

The Problem with this Case:

How could two Air Force officers, one of whom *is the weather forecaster*, not know a weather balloon when they saw one? Balloons always travel upward and in the direction of the prevailing wind, so how was it possible for a balloon to travel "back and forth over Stewart" *two or three times*, as well as stop, then move in an "up and down motion"?

My Conclusion: Burst that weather balloon theory.

Stewart Air Force Base, October 22, 1955

The only two pieces in this file are the record card and this letter sent from the Commander of the Eastern Air Defense Force at Stewart to the various Air Force Bases below, as well as the Director of Intelligence of the USAF in Washington, D.C.

```
FM COMDR EADF STEWART AFB NY

TO RJEDEN/COMDR ADC ENT AFB COLO

INFO RJEPNY/COMDR 26TH AIRDIV DEF ROSLYN AFSTA NY

RJEDUP/COMDR ATIC WRIGHT PATTERSON AFB O

RJEPHQ/DIRECTOR OF INTELL HQ USAF WASH DC
```

There is not much information in the following section of the letter, but apparently on the night of October 22, 1955, a civilian just north of Stewart AFB sighted a "silver to red" round object, the size of a "half dollar" held at arm's length. This witness called the base and appears to have spoken to an intelligence officer, who must have gone outside and also witnessed the object, which was visible for 30 minutes.

While it should have been an easy task for an intelligence officer to find out if a weather balloon had been released, and if it was still in the vicinity for half an hour, there is no mention if that information was obtained. In fact, the letter states that "No Further Info Available."

Without ascertaining whether or not there was even a balloon anywhere near Stewart AFB that night, the intelligence officer and the reporting officer dismissed the case as simply a weather balloon. Perhaps it was, but why not offer easily obtainable supporting evidence to prove it?

```
CIC 177 FLY OBRPT-BRIGHT SILVER TO RED, ROUND: SIZE HALF DOLLAR

1 OBJECT TIME 2214Z FOR 30 MIN DURATION, VISUAL SIGHTING FROM

STEWART AFB NORTH OF FIELD. OVSERVER REPORTED BY TELEPHONE TO EADF

INT. OFFICER- INT OFFICER ALSO SAW OBJECT. REPT BY ███████████

██████████ NEWBURGH NEW YORK. VISIBILITY UNLIMITED. PROBABLE

WEATHER BALLOON. NO FURTHER INFO AVAILABLE.
```

The following is not a Project Blue Book case, although it should have been! It is from an interview I conducted in 2013.

Member of the U.S. Air Force, Stewart Air Force Base, c. 1968

Since first beginning my research into the history of UFOs in the Hudson Valley, I wanted to personally speak to someone who had been at Stewart Air Force Base about any possible sightings or inexplicable radar contacts. Thanks to the Pine Bush UFO Festival in 2013, I finally found someone who was with the Air Force, stationed at Stewart in 1968-69. He had an amazing story to tell—and he would only tell it to me.

When I interviewed him by phone a few days later, he began by saying he worked at the SAGE building on the base. I asked what SAGE meant, and he told me it stood for Semi-Automatic Ground Environment, which still didn't make it any clearer! He then explained that it was a massive radar network and air defense system that stretched across the country.

The SAGE building at Stewart Airport in Newburgh is just across the street from the current terminal building. Many people see it every day, but few understand the important role it played.

According to the website of MIT's Lincoln Laboratory:

The scope of the SAGE Air Defense System, as it evolved from its inception in 1951 to its full deployment in 1963, was enormous. The cost of the project, both in funding and the number of military, civilian, and contractor personnel involved, exceeded that of the Manhattan Project...

The SAGE system, by the time of its full deployment, consisted of 100s of radars, 24 direction centers, and 3 combat centers spread throughout the U.S. The direction centers were connected to 100s of airfields and surface-to-air missile sites, providing a multilayered engagement capability. ...The direction centers automatically processed data from multiple remote radars, provided control information to intercepting aircraft and surface-to-air missile sites, and provided command and control and situational awareness displays to over 100 operator stations at each center. It was far and away the most grandiose systems engineering effort—and the largest electronic system-of-systems "ever contemplated."

According to a technical memo written in 1953 (by George Valley and Jay Forrester: Lincoln Laboratory Technical Memorandum No. 20, "A Proposal for Air Defense System Evolution: The Transition Phase."):

Briefly, the... system will consist of: (1) a net of radars and other data sources and (2) digital computers that (a) receive the radar and other information to detect and track aircraft, (b) process the track data to form a complete air situation, and (c) guide weapons to destroy enemy aircraft.

The MIT website further delineates the purpose of SAGE:

1. Early warning radar detects approaching aircraft
2. Radar reports automatically transmitted to direction center (DC) via phone lines
3. DC processes data
4. Air bases, HQs, and missile batteries notified
5. Data relayed between DC and adjoining centers
6. DC assigns interceptor aircraft and vectors interceptors to targets
7. Interceptors rendezvous with and intercept targets
8. DC informs HQ of results; missile batteries provide second line of defense if needed

Obviously, during the Cold War, it was imperative that the United States maintained a state-of-the-art early detection and defense system, as the possibility of a Soviet nuclear strike hung like a pall in the skies above America, and a critical part of that system was SAGE. And the reason I have gone into such detail about SAGE is to establish that as the fate of the free world rested in the hands of this defense network, it had to be ultra-reliable and accurate. Therefore, if something suspicious or inexplicable was detected, it would command immediate and serious attention.

Just such an incident *did* occur one night in 1968 or 1969. Something was traveling through east coast airspace at "a tremendous rate of speed," and "at an altitude where civilian and military aircraft traveled." Air Force personnel quickly ruled out a meteor or any other natural object. Due to its speed, they also ruled out *any manmade vehicle*. So, what exactly does that leave?

The SAGE system was checked and rechecked to make sure it was functioning properly. Then Air Force personnel at Stewart contacted other SAGE installations to see if they were also picking up this object, and it was confirmed that this incredible craft was being tracked by multiple locations.

The man I spoke to doesn't know if the Air Force initiated any response to this object racing through U.S airspace. Perhaps they did, or perhaps there wasn't even time to have a response, as the craft was moving so quickly. In any event, there was great excitement on the base that night, and "everyone continued to talk about that night for years."

This is an extremely important case, and not only in terms of Hudson Valley sightings. When Air Force personnel working at SAGE installations get excited by something—something they can't explain—that is a *very* big deal, and one with national consequences. Even with this single case, it proves that the military and the government know more than they are admitting—not that anyone is surprised by that, but it's certainly nice to have evidence to back that up!

I thanked this gentleman very much for sharing his story, and I would encourage other military personnel to also come forward to tell what they know.

Sad, but True!

I don't know who first made this "Air Force Identification Chart," but there are versions of it all over the Internet. I thought it was very apropos for the chapters containing Project Blue Book reports!

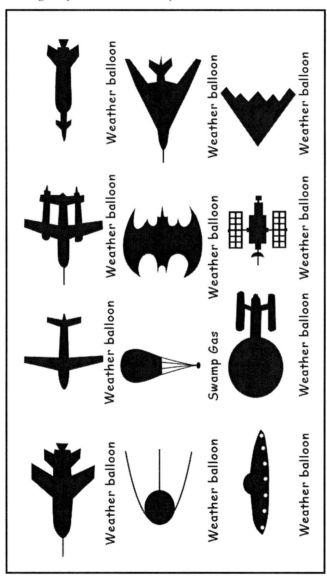

10
Project Blue Book: Hudson Valley

Walkill, NY, April 11, 1949

The following is testimony and a sketch made by an eyewitness in a letter sent to the Technical Intelligence Division of Wright Patterson Air Force base.

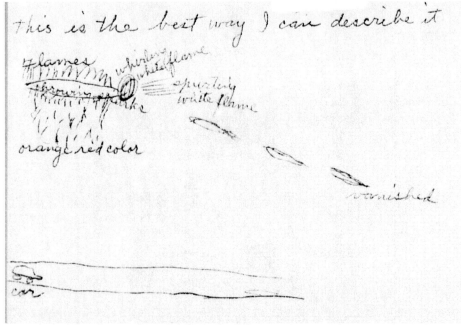

The notes on the sketch read: *Flames, throwing sparks, orange red color, whirling white flames, spurting white flames,* and *vanished.*

> *I was riding in the car with my husband and saw what I thought at first was a burning airplane, it was gliding in as if about to land.*
> *I sat spellbound for fully a minute staring at this flaming object when all at once it vanished. My husband did not see it as I did not want to take his attention from the*

wheel, when the object vanished, then I told him what I had seen, and wondered if someone else had seen that thing in the sky. A few days later I talked with a person who had seen it.

To me it looked like the framework of something burning.

I live in the Hudson Valley so this object probably disappeared behind a mountain.

I am a farmer's wife, hope this information may help you.

The official conclusion of this case was that the witness saw a meteor. (It is also misfiled under the heading of Toledo, Ohio.)

Peekskill, NY, July 22, 1949

On Friday July 22, at about 8:45 p.m., my wife and thirteen year old daughter, in the company of a young man, were walking on a country road immediately in the rear of our house on the outskirts of Peekskill, New York. They saw two flying discs. I did not see them myself, but have been waiting with camera in hand, hoping they might appear again. I called each one individually into a room and asked them to describe what they saw. Each one seemed to have seen exactly the same thing.

On the ground it was not quite dark but there were no stars visible in the sky as yet. However, the sun had set beyond the horizon. There was no red sun-set in the sky. The sky was blue with scattered clouds. These objects came whirling out of the southeast and traveled northwest. Both discs followed one another in exactly the same track across the sky. The three who saw them were looking in a southerly direction. They described them as follows:

The discs appeared to them to be slightly larger than a full moon. They were pure white and gave the appearance of having concaved depth. They were whirling, or spinning, in the same direction in which they were traveling, and at a terrific speed as if being rolled across the sky. The outer-rounded edge seemed solid, but not sharp, due to the whirling motion. The first disc seemed to have a bluish shadow in the center or was transparent, but the second one was solid white. They sped across the sky and disappeared behind a white cloud. The folks waited to see them come out of the cloud bank but they did not reappear. Either they dissolved in the cloud, or turned in a direction that they were obscured by the cloud. They had a rather eerie and awesome effect on the three who witnessed the spectacle.

The young man, (name blacked out) is the son of our Minister, Reverend Ernest F. Neumann of Port Chester, New York, and is a concert pianist of considerable reputation. When you know him, you would not doubt his veracity. He was the first to see them and he attracted the attention of my wife and daughter. Most certainly, my wife and thirteen year old daughter would have no reason to prevaricate. All three were out walking a new dog which we recently purchased for our daughter. These three are willing to give an oath to what they saw.

Another strange thing that has happened: W.L.N.A. our local radio station, is located on a hill opposite where our home is located. They leave the air at 8:00 p.m. every evening. That is about 45 minutes before the discs were seen. The cloud into which they disappeared was almost above the station's antenna. The station has not been functioning properly. However, it was supposed to be OK Saturday morning following the appearance of the discs.

[At this point he describes how several programs that were taped that weekend were badly distorted when played back, and the station engineer could not find the source of the problem, which predominantly seemed to affect the recording equipment and magnetic tapes.]

My thought in telling you this; could it be possible that these discs were electrical phenomenon of some sort that has magnetized the station's equipment and tapes, or is it some sort of atomic energy that is loose and loading things with active radio waves, or something designed to block radar? This is just a wild guess. If this same pattern has happened elsewhere, then it might add up to something.

Colonel Clingerman, Chief of the Analysis Division, Intelligence Department, responded to this man's letter. He stated that "the appearance of these objects" was similar to "plastic research balloons in flight," and that the "technical difficulties" at the radio station were "purely coincidental."

Did these three reliable witnesses simply see balloons? Were the subsequent problems with the magnetic tapes and equipment at the radio station just a coincidence? You, the reader, must decide.

Tallman, NY, July 28, 1949

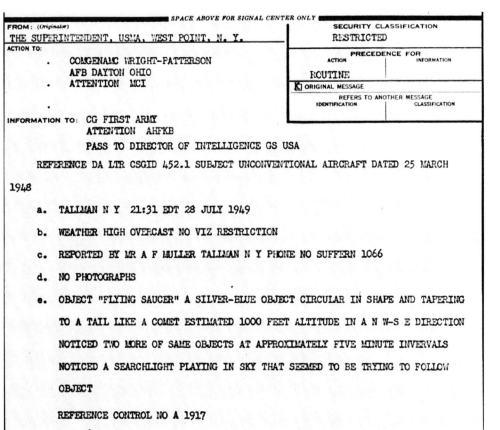

SPACE ABOVE FOR SIGNAL CENTER ONLY

FROM: (Originator)
THE SUPERINTENDENT, USMA, WEST POINT, N. Y.

SECURITY CLASSIFICATION
RESTRICTED

ACTION TO:
• COMGENAMC WRIGHT-PATTERSON
AFB DAYTON OHIO
• ATTENTION MCI

PRECEDENCE FOR
ACTION   INFORMATION
ROUTINE
☒ ORIGINAL MESSAGE

REFERS TO ANOTHER MESSAGE
IDENTIFICATION   CLASSIFICATION

INFORMATION TO: CG FIRST ARMY
ATTENTION AHFKB
PASS TO DIRECTOR OF INTELLIGENCE GS USA

REFERENCE DA LTR CSGID 452.1 SUBJECT UNCONVENTIONAL AIRCRAFT DATED 25 MARCH

1948

a. TALLMAN N Y 21:31 EDT 28 JULY 1949

b. WEATHER HIGH OVERCAST NO VIZ RESTRICTION

c. REPORTED BY MR A F MULLER TALLMAN N Y PHONE NO SUFFERN 1066

d. NO PHOTOGRAPHS

e. OBJECT "FLYING SAUCER" A SILVER-BLUE OBJECT CIRCULAR IN SHAPE AND TAPERING

TO A TAIL LIKE A COMET ESTIMATED 1000 FEET ALTITUDE IN A N W-S E DIRECTION

NOTICED TWO MORE OF SAME OBJECTS AT APPROXIMATELY FIVE MINUTE INVERVALS

NOTICED A SEARCHLIGHT PLAYING IN SKY THAT SEEMED TO BE TRYING TO FOLLOW

OBJECT

REFERENCE CONTROL NO A 1917

The conclusion of this case was that there was "Insufficient Data For Evaluation."

It's interesting to note that this report was sent by the Superintendent of West Point. I am also stunned that they didn't try to conclude that the three "flying saucers" were actually balloons!

White Plains, NY, June 28, 1953

At 6:02pm a pilot in route to Teterboro airport was flying a Luscombe aircraft at 1,500 feet when he observed a "circular (slightly elongated) dark object which appeared to be approx 6 ft in diameter traveled at an estimated 240 mph at approx 2,500 ft in NE direction."

The Project Blue Book conclusion was: "Although the description is similar to a weather balloon without a light, there is insufficient supporting data to determine the identity of the object."

As weather balloons can only travel horizontally at the prevailing wind speed, it is absurd to even consider that an object traveling at 240 mph at that altitude is a balloon.

White Plains, NY, July 17, 1952

This is one of those rare cases where the more I read, the harder it was to believe! The file is a whopping 19 pages filled with eyewitness descriptions and sketches. Normally, I would be thrilled with so much information, but after getting through all of the pages, I couldn't help but feel that I had just taken a very long ride on the Crazy Train.

I will not reproduce the complete file, as it would take up an entire chapter, but I will relate the pertinent information and let you decide. Is this one of the most remarkable sightings of all time in the Hudson Valley, or was this woman under the influence of drugs or alcohol?

The first page of the file is promising. The description is as follows:

> Two large "flying saucers" which made a whirring sound and were "flying on edge" observed by a woman in White Plains, N.Y.

Despite the abundance of eyewitness testimony, the conclusion was: "Insufficient Data for Evaluation, Unknown."

The personal information on the witness is that she was a 54-year-old housewife, and Civil Defense Day Post Warden. She had last attended school in 1914 at the Malden Business College in Malden, Massachusetts. She also mentioned she had since studied "art and portrait painting."

It was 3:10pm on a clear day, and she was "on a cot" in the yard when she heard what she at first thought were bombers—an engine sound similar to "the noise made by a small steamer, a muffled staccato." What at first appeared to be the propellers of a bomber at a distance, grew to the size of two Ferris wheels attached by a framework. Here is a description of her sighting in her own words:

They first appeared upon the scene like two small silver disks at that distance. I was lying on a cot facing North in the direction they were coming from. I thought at first these silver like disks were the propellers of a bomber, but it immediately dawned on me that propellers wouldn't be discernible at that great distance, so I kept my eyes focused on these two objects. Prior to their appearance I heard noise similar to the noise of bombers flying in formation, but a much softer smoother hum. Upon scanning the sky nothing could be seen, then presently silver disks appeared directly North and coming directly toward me in what seemed to be traveling in the orbit of the sun, traveling very smoothly and as though the two circles were attached. The circles were identical in shape (perfect circles) and identical in size and color. They were traveling constantly in an upright position and on an even keel. As they became larger I noticed the whole center of both circles were whirling and couldn't help but attribute the noise I was hearing to the whirling appearance in the center of circles. The whirling appearance reminded me of the nickel plated blades revolving in an electric fan, and revolving at a terrific speed. The rim of circles were of a dazzling blue white crystal, almost like diamonds, but this rim did not seem to be revolving. When this twin object disappeared at its largest size, making a right angle turn I noticed the circles appeared to have a rectangular framework behind them. I saw only the top bar and the left hand corner. This framework seemed of a dull pale gray material..

Impressive description, and quite a detailed. She also wrote:

Again, I have no meansof determining how many miles an hour these twin objects were traveling. The only thing I can say to give you an idea, is that it took about sixty seconds for these twin objects to travel between the two points I observed them to travel in. I couldn't have been in a better spot to view these circles, and only wish that a scientist could have had the opportunity I had.

It was the most beautiful sight, more breath taking than any planets to be seen with the naked eye. It made a profound impression on me, and a day doesn't go by that I don't find myself dwelling on that most unusual celestial apparition.

Could I have been witnessing a couple of planets doing an epicycle they speak of in Ptolemaic astronomy?

I have never studied astronomy, but common sense tells me there would be no framework to account for, noise or a right angle turn.

The line above about possibly "witnessing a couple of planets doing an epicycle they speak of in Ptolemaic astronomy," really threw me. Why on earth would she write that if what she saw were two massive, whirling crystalline spheres attached by a bar? I was also uneasy with one of her responses on the forms, that if it wasn't for that bar and the sounds, she would have thought they were "a token of Heaven."

There is another letter from this woman in the file, and it begins with the following:

In reporting the Twin Objects I sighted July 17 from my back yard, I purposely withheld one very important feature as I couldn't bring myself to reveal such an astounding feature. I had kept this particular feature a very dark secret for one whole month, when I felt I could do so no longer. Therefore, on August 18 I made an appointment with the pastor of our church, bringing all correspondence I had had with your Intelligence Center for him to read. I then told him the secret, and asked him if he thought I did right in withholding this information. He replied, by saying he thought I had given enough information for the time being, as it sounded so unbelievable, and added smilingly - "At least we know they are not Russians."

And what was this "very dark secret" she withheld in her other reports? She also heard voices...

In Figure 11, as per my sketch, this Twin Object took a sudden upswing and in this practically upended position the most astounding features were revealed. First I noticed attachments and gadgets down in between the framework (which I now think was housing for beings aboard) and spheres, and then above the hum and staccato thump I was hearing, I distinctly heard voices greatly amplified, that seemed to come from beings similar to ourselves. It was as though a door of a large auditorium had been opened the instant the Object took this sudden upswing on a group of eight to ten people conversing with one another in a slow quiet manner, seemingly unaware that their voices were being heard down here below. The vocal tones were beautiful, and all seemed to be of the same quality with no guttural or nasal sounds. They were all of a middle range, more like mature feminine voices than masculine. No harsh consonants were audible, and the vowels were well rounded, open and long. If consonants were used they were not heard. I never heard a language on this earth as beautiful. I grant you, I haven't heard all languages spoken, but I have heard several.

She then concludes that if she is allowed to write an article about her sighting, she will not include the part about the voices "as I don't think the public is ready for such a revelation." But she simply could not hold back this secret any longer, because if she was the only person in the world to hear those voices, science would have been at a loss if she hadn't revealed the truth.

She did produce some excellent sketches (below), both close-ups of the two circles, and the relative sizes and path they took, concluding that when they disappeared it was like "into a slit in the sky."

There are obviously some very compelling features to this case, but just as obviously there are some red flags. I recommend that you read the entire case file, which would be listed under White Plains for July of 1952. Project Blue Book archives are available through several websites.

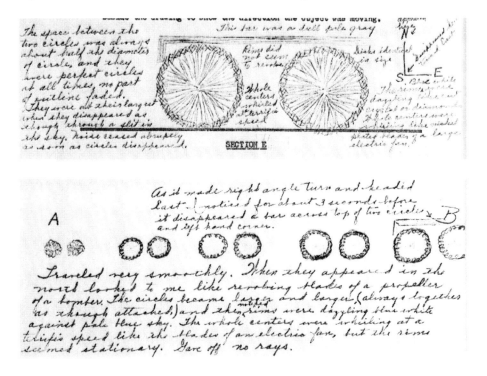

Captain Edson Wood, Hyde Park, NY, October 2, 1955

At 6:16pm on October 2, 1955, Captain Edson Wood was piloting a DC-3 for Colonial Airlines, Flight 27, in route to LaGuardia Airport, at an altitude of about 6,000 feet over Hyde Park. Winds were light, conditions were clear, and visibility was unlimited. Wood was 33 years old, and had served in the AAF (Army Air Forces) during WWII. He was obviously quite familiar with aircraft and the night sky, and would not have made an official report about his sighting unless he was certain it was something remarkable and out of the ordinary.

Of course, in its infinite wisdom, Project Blue Book took only a few words of Captain Wood's statement and concluded the bright "blue-white light" was "Typical of a shooting star." As always, it's up to you to review the evidence and decide for yourself. The following is part of the official statement, personally handwritten by Wood on the Blue Book forms.

Out of the corner of my eye I noticed what appeared to be a bright meteor or shooting star. As I called it to the attention of my co-pilot, it reduced its speed to that of ours [approx. 170mph] *and paralleled our course, for roughly 15 seconds. It then took off in a southeasterly direction and gained altitude at a seemingly infinite speed finally disappearing from sight in approx. another 15 sec. time interval.*

Although I am not at all certain what it was, I am reasonably certain it was not a star, a jet or conventional aircraft, or an illusion. I tried unsuccessfully to contact Air Defense radar in hopes they might track this object.

Captain Wood immediately reported his sighting to Colonial Airlines when he landed at LaGuardia. The following day, a representative of the airlines wrote a letter to the Chief of Staff of the Air Force, asking, "If possible, we would be very interested in what the object was and if there is any way we can prevent future occurrences." They also included a typed statement from Wood describing the object.

In that statement, obviously composed within 24 hours of the sighting, Wood writes that "A brilliant blue-white light resembling a meteor passed abeam of our port side and hovered approximately 10 to 15 seconds. This object then departed on a southeasterly direction at an extreme rate of speed and disappeared from sight. As it faded from sight it appeared to gain altitude. Its speed and altitude were difficult to estimate."

Subsequently on the Blue Book forms, Captain Wood goes into greater detail about the sighting. The object appeared to be the size of a baseball held at arm's length. He also specified that it changed speed from "170mph to infinity," and changed course and altitude as well—obviously not characteristics of a meteor. In Section 20 of the form, he made the following sketches illustrating how the object veered upward, as well as the shape of the craft.

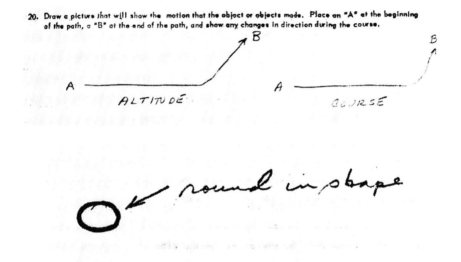

20. Draw a picture that will show the motion that the object or objects made. Place an "A" at the beginning of the path, a "B" at the end of the path, and show any changes in direction during the course.

ALTITUDE

COURSE

round in shape

This case is an excellent example of a gem buried beneath piles of Blue Book disinformation and misinformation. Project reporters constantly employed the technique of taking a couple of words from the witnesses and miscategorizing the entire sighting—Wood said it initially looked like a shooting star, so it is branded simply as a shooting star.

Never mind that a highly trained airline pilot who served in the Army Air Forces in WWII, along with his copilot, witnessed a round object slow down to keep pace with their plane, then accelerate to a tremendous speed and travel upward at a sharp angle and finally disappear from view. Meteors do not slow down to an aircraft's exact speed, then go back up into the sky. Perhaps some type of secret military vehicle would have been capable of this behavior, but no such explanation was offered to Colonial Airlines—at least not one that appears in the file.

I tend to believe that in 1955 the U.S. Air Force did not have round aircraft that emitted a brilliant blue-white light that could hover next to an aircraft going 170mph, and could also accelerate at a rate of speed that even two pilots couldn't estimate. I also believe that the SAGE radar facility at Stewart AFB (see previous chapter) had its beady little eyes glued to that object and tracked it over its entire course through U.S. air space. And finally, I firmly believe we will never be able to prove any of this thanks to the evasive maneuvers of Project Blue Book.

A postcard image of a Colonial Airlines DC-3. Colonial was acquired by Eastern Airlines in 1956.

Greenwood Lake, NY, July 14, 1956

A man by the name of White, who lived in New York City and was a portrait painter, called the Air Force Office of Special Investigations in Manhattan to report a sighting that he, his wife, and another couple had at Greenwood Lake. The following are excerpts from the file. Because White was later reluctant to be interviewed in person by Air Force personnel because it "would take too much time," his case was labeled as being in the "insufficient data category but with the strong possibility of a hoax," even though he supplied his name and address, along with the names and address of the other couple, who were also interviewed.

White reported that on 14 July 1956 he had twice observed a flying object in the sky. The observations took place for short periods at about 1630 hours and 2200 hours. The periods of observation were brief. White could not tell whether he had seen the same object in both instances of observation. He described the object seen at 1630 hours as the size of a dime, silver colored, disc shape, and motionless; then it tilted, appeared to have a dome on the top, and disappeared. The object seen at night was also the size of a dime, red in color, of disc shape, and was traveling at high speed; it curved sharply across the sky, and disappeared. Weather conditions were good for observation, no instruments were used. (Name blacked out) advised that his wife (name and address blacked out), both of Greenwood Lake, New York, could corroborate his observation, in part. When asked if he could be interviewed, replied that a personal interview would take too much of his time.

Tarrytown, NY, August 9, 1956

This particular file only contained two entries; this single paragraph and the index card. I guess they couldn't get their stories straight, as the reporting officer claimed it was a shooting star, the reviewing officer said it was a weather balloon, and someone else wrote in that it was Mars—any one of which a WWII pilot with a commercial license should have recognized!

Case 183, Tarrytown, N.Y., Aug. 9, 1956—At 12:15 police headquarters received a phone call from Walter Kocher who saw a mysterious light in the sky. Sgt. Fintan Maegerle was dispatched by radio to investigate. He confirmed the report together with two other officers. Sgt. Maegerle, a World War II pilot who holds a commercial license, described the light as yellowish, and "five to eight times the size of any star in the sky." He could not estimate its altitude, but said it was moving in jerks in a generally southeasterly direction. In his flying experience he had seen nothing like it. . . . About 1:30 a.m., the light disappeared.[9]

AISS-UFOB-218-56

1. DATE	2. LOCATION	12. CONCLUSIONS
8/25 Aug 56	Tarrytown, N. Y.	☒ Was Balloon ☐ Probably Balloon ☐ Possibly Balloon
3. DATE-TIME GROUP	4. TYPE OF OBSERVATION	☐ Was Aircraft ☐ Probably Aircraft ☐ Possibly Aircraft
09/0415Z Aug 56	☒ Ground-Visual ☐ Ground-Radar ☐ Air-Visual ☐ Air-Intercept Radar	
5. PHOTOS ☐ Yes ☒ No	6. SOURCE Civilian	☐ Was Astronomical MARS ☐ Probably Astronomical ☐ Possibly Astronomical
7. LENGTH OF OBSERVATION Still visible at time of Initial report	8. NUMBER OF OBJECTS One (1)	9. COURSE Southeast	☐ Other_____ ☐ Insufficient Data for Evaluation ☐ Unknown
10. BRIEF SUMMARY OF SIGHTING One (1) yellow star-like object, 5 or 6 times the size of the North Star. Noticed because of light plus movement. Object moved very slowly in a southeasterly direction at a very high altitude. Object still in sight at time of initial report.		11. COMMENTS Do not concur with Reporting Officer that sighting was a shooting star. Sighting meets all criteria for a balloon hypothesis. Winds correlate to course of object. Evaluation of this headquarters as "was balloon."	

South Salem, NY, August 25, 1956

The reporting witness was a 60-year-old woman, who saw this object with her husband. The official Blue Book conclusion was that this was an aircraft. Perhaps the military was testing a missile, but it certainly doesn't sound like any conventional aircraft. The following are sketches and excerpts from the forms she filled out.

The best I can do is to say that it would be of a real bright, highly polished brass, somewhat in the shape of a bullet but tapered at both ends. As for the size I'd have no idea. it did not appear to be as large as the average airliner. more perhaps like a jet. or DC-4

120

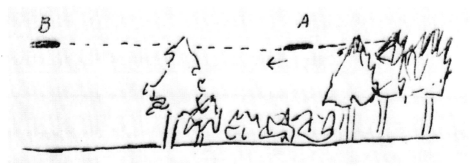

exhaust - vapor trail

The vapor trail stretched clear across the sky
and was real bright for the first 1/3 way.

B   A

38. In your opinion what do you think the object was and what might have caused it?

I have no idea. I do know it was no ordinary aircraft as
I live in an area where commercial planes, jets, and Army
planes pass daily regularly, da. and night, and none has ever
appeared like this. Furthermore, all of those have an accompanying
noise, no matter how distant - but this was completely silent.
They also have riding lights which blink on and off. This whole thing
glowed steadily from end to end.

West Nyack, NY, July 24, 1958

As an amateur astronomer, I have watched many meteors and meteor showers. However, I have yet to see a meteor that was metallic silver and the size of the full moon. Also, the witness was an engineer.

1. DATE	2. LOCATION	12. CONCLUSIONS
24 Jul 58	West Nyalk, New York	☐ Was Balloon ☐ Probably Balloon ☐ Possibly Balloon
3. DATE-TIME GROUP Local _____ GMT __24/1100Z__	**4. TYPE OF OBSERVATION** X☒ Ground-Visual ☐ Ground-Radar ☐ Air-Visual ☐ Air-Intercept Radar	☐ Was Aircraft ☐ Probably Aircraft ☐ Possibly Aircraft
5. PHOTOS ☐ Yes XXNo	**6. SOURCE** Civilian	☒X Was Astronomical Meteor ☐ Probably Astronomical ☐ Possibly Astronomical
7. LENGTH OF OBSERVATION 8-10 secs	**8. NUMBER OF OBJECTS** one	**9. COURSE** West	☐ Other_____ ☐ Insufficient Data for Evaluation ☐ Unknown

10. BRIEF SUMMARY OF SIGHTING	11. COMMENTS
Obj moving East to West appeared to be about size of the full moon, shining a silver metallic color, no visible vapor trail. Shape slightly eliptical. Long axix in direction of flight. In sight for 8-10 secs & obj disappeared fm sight in Western sky.	Meteor sighting.

ATIC FORM 329 (REV 26 SEP 52)

Poughkeepsie (or Highland?), NY, August 25, 1962

A civilian observer "3 miles north of Poughkeepsie, NY near where routes 44 and 55 intersect 9W" observed a "fire-red" object the relative size of baseball held at arm's length, with a fiery tail. The object moved from an angle of about 90 degrees in the north sky, down to treetop level, then back up. The object also moved from side-to-side several times over the course of an hour.

Stewart AFB was contacted and they reported that "they had nothing in the area."

The Project Blue Book conclusion was that the "Small size and duration indicate it was an astronomical body. Sudden rising indicated by refraction as body sets. Both Vega & Deneb (stars) were in the area indicated at the time of initial sighting."

Granted, one hour is a long sighting, but since when is an object with the apparent size of a baseball considered small? And how many stars look as big as baseballs?

Note: The recorded location is incorrect. Routes 44 and 55 intersect with Route 9W on the other side of the Hudson River from Poughkeepsie, by the town of Highland.

Scarsdale, NY, July 31 and August 6, 1963

A 37-year-old woman wrote a letter to the "Headquarters of the Air Force, Pentagon, UFO Division." The following is an excerpt.

```
At the suggestion of a gentleman at the Airforce Information
Center in New York City, I am writing to you regarding a
phenomenon observed by me and five other persons last night
(July 31) in the sky above my home in Scarsdale, N. Y. This
was at about eleven o'clock in the evening.

The object was shaped like two cones joined at their bases,
flying at about five to ten thousand feet.  It appeared to
be approximately the size of a large airplane moving through
the sky at the same rate and in the same manner as a plane
in a northwesterly direction.  It was all aglow as if made
of light.  It disappeared from our sight in a few minutes.
Besides the six of us who saw this object at the same time,
I have not found anyone else in this area who also observed
it.
```

When filling out the official report forms, she also described the glow of the object as being orange, and that it was spinning. The same craft was observed again on August 6th.

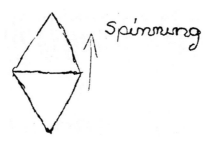

Despite the fact the six people witnessed this glowing, orange, spinning, double cone-shaped object, the official conclusion was that there was "Nothing conflicting with the a/c analysis," so it "was probably an aircraft."

Grace Dutcher, Middletown, NY, 1963

I read an article in the Medical Tribune which says you are still interested in flying objects in the sky.

I would like to tell you what I saw. About 2 years ago I was looking at the sky from my bedroom window. It was one of those nights when the sky was a carpet of stars and in the northwest near the horizon I saw what I at first thought were falling stars but then I realized they were brighter than stars and were darting in all directions. I watched for about maybe 20 or 30 seconds and then they all darted into a formation like this-

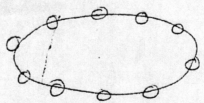

They were perfectly spaced in this formation and stayed in this position for I should say about 30 seconds, then one by one they flew north near the horizon at a tremendous speed, they were all out of signt in just a few seconds. I am not sure of the number, perhaps there were 8 or 10. All this I saw very plainly, about 9:30 or 10 o'clock at night.

Unfortunately, there was no follow-up interview, as the sighting happened during the summer of 1963, and Dutcher did not send this letter until August of 1965. The official record of her case has the following:

10. CONCLUSION

UNIDENTIFIED

Report received two years after observation. Too old to warrant additional investigation. No apparent soultion.

Interesting side notes to this case:

I decided to see if it was possible that Grace Dutcher was still alive, so I did a search. I found that while she lived to the amazing age of 101, she had passed away in 2002.

Also, you have to love a time when you could send a letter about your sighting and this was all you needed to put on the envelope:

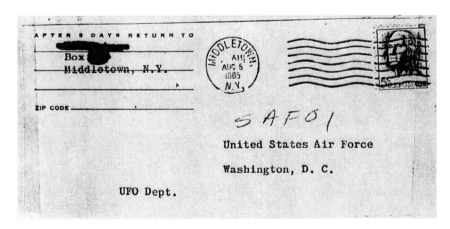

White Plains, NY, December 10, 1963

At 2:30am, a woman woke up to a "vibrating sensation" in her ears. She ran to the bathroom window which looked due east and saw "a very bright light, yellow in color with sharp rays of light shooting out in all directions."

She ran to get her glasses and when she returned several seconds later, the object was now a dull yellow disk that was descending. As the disk went lower, a bright crescent shape appeared at the bottom, and then it went out of sight. There was "no smoke, and no exhaust trails or vapor

125

trail." The entire sighting lasted about 38 seconds, as timed by the second hand on her clock.

This was not her first reported sighting. In her letter and on her forms, she mentioned another experience eleven years earlier on July 17, 1952, when she saw "two attached spheres that were immense" and looked like they were made of crystal. That rang one huge bell, and checking the dates I realized it was the same woman who had written the very detailed and bizarre report of her sighting that appears earlier in this chapter. Does this add more or less credibility to her as a witness? Without personally interviewing someone, it's hard say.

What we can say is that Dr. Hynek must have personally reviewed this case, as the conclusion box of the report form also has a handwritten note which reads, "Dr. Hynek Considers Moon." While there was a crescent moon in the east at that time, the description of something falling straight down and out of sight in 38 seconds hardly makes that the likely explanation, and does nothing to address the vibration the witness experienced.

The official conclusion was that "the logical cause" was that "of a flare dropped by an airplane," although they concede that the "source of the flare is unknown."

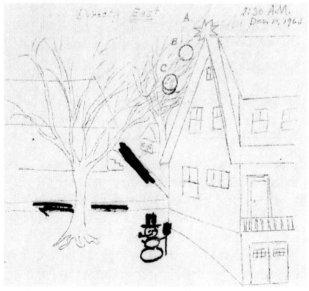

Finally, there is the sketch that the witness produced, which very nicely shows her perspective of the stages of object and the houses in the neighborhood. Please note that whoever was blacking out the street names also decided to draw in a snowman—which just goes to show how seriously they took these reports.

Monticello, NY, July 22, 1965

This is of particular interest as it is one of the earliest reports of a triangular-shaped craft in the area. The witness was a 13-year-old boy, who was categorized as a "Student and Amateur Astronomer" with "Reliability – Above average for age." He was outside on the night of July 22nd with his 600x telescope at a location about two miles south of Monticello when he saw something unusual moving from north to south.

Unfortunately, there is no direct statement by the witness in the file, just the summary of the important points of the observation, which are as follows:

1. The UFO was triangular in shape.
2. The UFO was the size of a pea to the eye, the size of a nickel in a 6 power telescope. (Note: It was actually the viewfinder of the telescope.)
3. The object was white to the eye. The object had a red nose, and a white body with a bright light aft in the scope.
4. There was one UFO.
5. N/A
6. Lines on front and port of nose.
7. A bright light, like a "sparkler aft."

Further description:

"The UFO was at an angle of 40˚ to 50˚ above the horizon when sighted first. It reappeared at an angle of 5-10˚ above horizon."

"The UFO faded out near vertical and passed over the horizon second sighting."

"Zigzag, or like lights flashing on aircraft wings tips. The UFO went from North to South, then passed from East to West near Southern horizon. It moved faster than a satellite and unlike a meteorite. It moved too fast to be observed in any but the finder scope of observer's astronomical telescope."

"The UFO was first visible for less than two minutes, then reappeared about 20 minutes later for about five minutes."

At the bottom of the report is the Preliminary Analysis, which states, "I feel that Mr. (name blacked out) perhaps observed a weather balloon. This area is quite near J-63 and other main jet routes to New York City.

Hugenot Vortac is about 20NM South of there and is the intersection jet routes J-63, J-7, and J-95."

The final conclusion reiterated that there are four major jet routes in the area, but the report itself admits that "Air traffic was light." It also says that weather balloons had been released in Albany and Kennedy airport, but the balloon theory was apparently dropped for the final conclusion, which was surprisingly noncommittal for a PBB case:

"No data presented to indicate that the objects could NOT have been A/C (aircraft)."

What was also surprising is the letter in the file from Major Quintanilla, head of Project Blue Book, who wrote to the Stewart Air Force base to obtain confirmation that the date of the observation of this triangular craft was indeed July 22, 1965. This is not typical for a Blue Book case, and it is interesting to note. Was this just a procedure to correct some clerical error? Also, if this was just a sighting of an aircraft or weather balloon, why would the head of the project request confirmation of the date?

Menands, NY, August 11, 1965

This woman's story is my personal favorite in terms of sticking it to the Air Force and giving them a piece of her mind!

Menands is a small town just north of Albany on the Hudson River. In 1965, a woman was sitting on her porch one summer evening, and at 7:25pm, she noticed that the birds were acting agitated. Looking up, she saw two silver, metallic objects flying low, traveling from north to south along the river. They made no sound, emitted no exhaust, and moved along together, except for a short "dip" one of the objects made, but then returned to the side of the other object. The following is a sketch that was made of these unique objects.

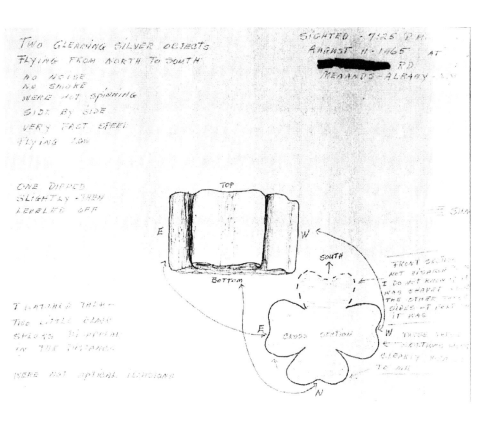

The observer was alarmed by the sight, but not because she thought they were alien spacecraft. In fact, she did not believe that there was life on other planets. She was concerned because she thought they were Russians vehicles, possibly launched from ships at sea, spying on us. With a mixture of Cold War fear and patriotic fervor, she called the Watervliet Arsenal and wanted to speak to the commanding officer. She never got through to him directly, but through some intermediary he told her it was just "an optical illusion."

An Albany newspaper picked up on her story, publishing both the sketch and her description, as well as including the conclusion that such objects simply did not exist. Infuriated that no one was paying attention to what she perceived as a serious threat to national security, she wrote a letter to the "U.S. Air Force, Chief of Staff, Dept. of Defense, Pentagon, Washington, D.C." and really let him have it. After describing in detail what she saw, she leveled this criticism directly at the "smug and careless government" and "Champagne sipping" military top brass:

Most Americans keep their eyes glued to T.V. or to the road. It is only the squares that ever look up. But squares can be patriotic and concerned about the security of their country, also. It is a mighty smug and careless government that will not be concerned and alarmed at all these reports.

These Champagne sipping, high and mighty men in charge of our security, that think they know it all, merely pass these reports off as crackpot.

Someday and maybe not too far in the future, when the Champagne glasses are knocked out of their hands and it is already too late-, they will say, " We should have listened and we should have believed."

She clearly expected a nuclear attack from the Russians, not an invasion from aliens. In fact, in her Blue Book forms she filled out, she relates that she was contacted by Major Donald Keyhoe of NICAP, who sent her information about UFOs. However, she reiterates that she still doesn't "believe in objects from outer space or from other planets."

My favorite lines come from those forms, where she states in no uncertain terms:

I saw something strange that <u>must</u> be investigated. If they are secret missiles our own government is testing, then I think I deserve some sort of explanation, because I saw them.

If they are not ours, then the U.S.A.F. had better get on the ball.

You go girl! How many UFO witnesses would like to stand on the steps of the U.S. Capitol building and shout the very same thing?

And what was the result of all these forms, letters, newspaper articles, and sketches? For all of this woman's efforts, her official Blue Book report card simply states:

Conclusion: Aircraft

Yonkers, NY, August or September, 1965

Other than the project record card, this letter and a small newspaper clipping were the only pieces in the file. The letter was written by a married woman living in Yonkers, who did not report the sighting until March of 1966, and she therefore could not remember the exact date of when the sighting occurred.

Here follows the particulars concerning an object seen in the sky as I was putting empty milk bottles outside my front door. It was seen in late August or early September, 1965, at about 9P.M.

1. *From the way the small lights arranged around it, it appeared to be BEETLE SHAPED.*
2. *Red and white small lights around it flickered on and off.*
3. *Two brilliantly lighted discs formed the face of it, placed side by side...like an enormous pair of eyes. The thick rims were red, the center portion amber.*
4. *The light of them was STEADY.*
5. *No apparent SOUND.*
6. *Heading SOUTH; almost directly toward my house.*
7. *Low altitude; about where a helicopter might fly looking for forest fires. And, the same degree of speed as a helicopter.*
8. *When it was above the area between the two houses across the street, it turned, and went off in the same direction from where it came.*

Comment: I do not deliberately look for flying objects; it was there and I SAW IT. It has been described in the enclosed clipping by an observer, as having two "eyes", like coins. The "eyes" that I saw were about the size of a car's headlights. They did indeed form the WHOLE FACE OF IT.

The clipping that she enclosed reads (the quality was so poor it was difficult to make out the name):

"One of the girls, An(?) (???)per, had a pair of binoculars. Through them, she made out a rim illuminated by the two red "eyes" she believes

131

she saw. She interpreted the shape to be disc-like, like a coin from the little she could make out. "I saw a rim, with two red lights in it, like eyes that case a red glow."

Unfortunately, there's no date or indication what newspaper this appeared in, but it is extremely important as it elevates this case from a single eyewitness to multiple eyewitnesses—an addition of several girls, one of whom got a close look at the object through a pair of binoculars. This information in not included on the project record card, which states there was only one witness, with no mention of binoculars. The official conclusion is as follows:

Object was probably an aircraft. However the sighting is carried as insufficient data because the observer does not remember the date of the sighting and the duration of the sighting.

Of course, not remembering the date or duration has nothing to do with the validity of the sighting, but this was PBB's way of effortlessly dismissing a unique and intriguing multiple-witness case.

Middletown, NY, September 6, 1965

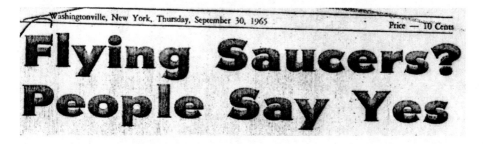

Washingtonville, New York, Thursday, September 30, 1965   Price — 10 Cents

Flying Saucers? People Say Yes

This is a case that actually made it into the newspaper, the *Orange County Post*, due in part, no doubt, because the editor of the newspaper was also a witness! There were apparently dozens of witnesses, including policemen, throughout the area during this September 6th sighting.

The witness who made the Blue Book report was a businessman, H. Kenneth Bayne. Through 30-power binoculars, he was able to determine that the rotating lights everyone saw were part of a "circular disc shaped object with a dome on the bottom."

The Blue Book conclusion, based upon observations made the *following night* by a local chemistry and astronomy professor, was that the object was simply the star Arcturus. And even though a plane was sent from Stewart AFB and was observed making "a pass at the object," there is no mention of it in the report.

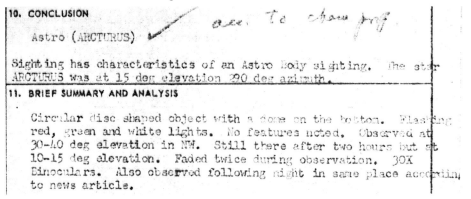

10. CONCLUSION

Astro (ARCTURUS)

Sighting has characteristics of an Astro Body sighting. The star ARCTURUS was at 15 deg elevation 290 deg azimuth.

11. BRIEF SUMMARY AND ANALYSIS

Circular disc shaped object with a dome on the bottom. Flashing red, green and white lights. No features noted. Observed at 30-40 deg elevation in NW. Still there after two hours but at 10-15 deg elevation. Faded twice during observation. 30X Binoculars. Also observed following night in same place according to news article.

The following is the article in the *Orange County Post*, which appeared September 30, 1965.

WASHINGTONVILLE. (OCP) - - Over the past week, dozens of people throughout Orange County have claimed they've seen flying saucer objects in the sky. Officials at Stewart Air Force Base in Newburgh have started an investigation.

Many people naturally are skeptical. They ask "Who are these people that have seen the objects, and how do we know they're not exaggerating?"

The truth of the matter is, too many people have seen the objects, including businessmen, policemen and other responsible citizens.

One such person is H. Kenneth Bayne a Middletown business executive, who lives at 18 Crescent Place.

Bayne and a group of neighbors watched the object hovering in the sky for close to two hours Sunday night, beginning around 9. On Monday night, Bayne's wife Sally saw the object again.

133

"I observed the object through binoculars," Bayne said. "It was a disc-shaped relolving object hovering above. It was noticeable at night because of the green, red, and white spinning lights."

Bayne said the lights resembled the spinning top light of a patrol car. He said at one point, the object seemed to be at a 45 degree angle.

Watching the object in a sort of circus-show with six other neighbors and some children Bayne said the object did not move at one point for about 20 minutes.

He said one of the neighbors called Stewart Air Force Base, and within a half-hour an aircraft approached and appeared to be on a collision course with the flying saucer object.

The plane, however, appeared to make a pass at the object and then flew away. When Bayne and his wife left at 11 p.m., the object was still visible.

Bayne who served in the Air Force, said he would discount the object was a star because it seemed to disappear and then reappear. He said he didn't think it was a reflection but obviously a "solid mass."

Bayne said he saw many planes in the air Sunday afternoon, of the "flying Boxcar" type, which are heavy aircraft, and wondered if they had anything to do with the nightime activity of the flying objects — or saucers, or whatever it was.

Bayne said he had an interest in the reports about flying saucers, and was naturally curious. He said, however, he was "thankful" he was not alone when he observed the object at length. He said it was something he has never seen before.

Bayne's wife watched the object Monday night, and reported it moved positions drastically.

Bayne asked an unresolved question: "What if they are vehicles with beings? Why have they not tried to communicate?"

Dr. Walter F. Gard, a chemistry and astronomy professor, set up a telescope at Orange County Community College Monday night, and after viewing objects, announced they were stars.

Officials at Stewart Air Force Base, however did not announce they were stars. An official made no other comment except to say an investigation is being held.

Saugerties, NY, January 1966

1. DATE - TIME GROUP	2. LOCATION
16 January 66 16/0800Z	42.04N 73.56W (Saugerties, New York)
3. SOURCE	10. CONCLUSION
Civilian	Astro (JUPITER)
4. NUMBER OF OBJECTS One large, possibly Three smaller	Jupiter RA 5.23, Mag -2.2. Setting at 0400 local.
5. LENGTH OF OBSERVATION	11. BRIEF SUMMARY AND ANALYSIS
1 Hour, 30 Minutes	Observer saw a white, football shaped object. There was one
6. TYPE OF OBSERVATION	large object and possibly three smaller objects moving out of
Ground-Visual	the large object and off to the West. Sighted the object at 30 deg elevation in the Northwest and it disappeared to the
7. COURSE	West by fading from sight.
Northwest	
8. PHOTOS	
☐ Yes ☒ No	
9. PHYSICAL EVIDENCE	
☐ Yes ☒ No	

FORM
FTD SEP 63 0-329 (TDE) Previous editions of this form may be used.

This project record indicates that the civilian witnesses saw the planet Jupiter. Granted, an observation time of one hour and thirty minutes is suspicious, but then so is the content in the rest of the file.

The witnesses were a 30-year-old writer for IBM, and a-30-year-old housewife, probably his wife. What first attracted their attention to the bright white object was "its movement," which apparently was to the west, then it returned to its original position to the northwest, and repeated these movements—something Jupiter is not known for doing. They also described it as being football-shaped, and the size of a dime held at arm's length, also not indicative of a planet.

Then there is the fact that they saw "three smaller objects moving out of the larger object and off to the west." Jupiter does have moons, but they are too small to be seen with the naked eye, and none of them have been known to take off! The full report also states that these three smaller objects exhibited exhaust trails—again, not a feature of the Jovian satellites.

135

The report also states that the weather was clear, with no cloud cover, and visibility of 12 miles. It also says that there was a temperature inversion at 14,000 feet, which is a layer of warmer air over a colder air mass. Based on that, the reporting officer, Lt. Thomas Waller of Stewart Air Force Base, concluded:

"I believe that the UFO seen by these people may have been a phenomenon of the temperature inversion."

Essentially, he claims that this bright object which moved back and forth across the sky several times and released three objects that moved away and left exhaust trails, was nothing more than an optical illusion of the planet Jupiter.

Near the end of the report, he mentions something that one would think would be important enough to include on the initial report record, which just states that the witness was a "Civilian."

Lt. Waller adds:

"New York State Police confirm the sighting—two patrolmen saw the objects."

This certainly adds some weight to the case, with two State Police officers obviously seeing not one, but multiple "objects."

The last line of the report says that there may be photographic evidence which will be provided if something shows up after the film is developed, but there is no further mention of photos in the report.

Of course, for those who have grown cynical from Project Blue Book half-truths and untruths, this doesn't mean there wasn't valid photographic evidence produced.

Marlboro, NY, January 20, 1966

At 10:30pm, a 26-year-old technician employed at International Nickel was driving on Route 9W, two miles north of Marlboro. Some unusual lights caught his attention, and upon looking more closely, he saw a narrow, circular object "about the size of a medicine ball" held at arm's length. There were two bright, "red and green rotating lights on the backend of the object." There wasn't any sound or exhaust trail, and when it was first sighted, it was only between a quarter to a half mile away, and about 500 feet above the Hudson River.

(Note: To put this sighting in context, a medicine ball is roughly the size of a beach ball. If the witness statement was accurate, this would have been an extremely large object.)

He saw this craft initially heading south, and then it turned and went north, flying a somewhat rectangular pattern over the river. The entire sighting lasted about two or three minutes.

The officer at Stewart AFB who prepared the report stated, "It is my opinion that the observer saw an aircraft in a holding pattern for a landing at a local airfield."

Wappingers Falls, NY, Spook Hill Road, March-April, 1966

This possibly represents one of the worst Project Blue Book lies— which is saying a lot! The official project record form dismisses this case with the brief and simple conclusion of "Astro (METEOR)." After looking at the witness' sketch and reading the following, you'll see just how ridiculous and insulting was this meteor excuse.

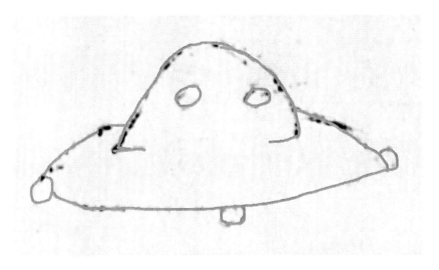

(Note: The PBB copy quality of the sketch was so poor that I traced the outlines to make it easier to see. I did not include the second sketch of the neighborhood and streets around Spook Hill Road.)

K. Position, Title and Comments of Preparing Officer:

Lt. T. S. Waller
NAV/EWO
4713th Def Sys Eval Sq
Stewart AFB, NY

I feel that aircraft might possibly account for some of these sightings, but certainly not all.

Mrs. ███████ reports having seen many UFO's every night, except 2 or 3, since 31 March 1966. The objects appear to be red lights and follow a smooth flight path when changing altitudes. They fly at various altitudes and follow various flight paths, appearing in all quadrants from the observers home; several flying in the same area simultaneously but not in formation.

On the evening of 25 April at approximately 2130L, Mrs. ███████ went up the hill behind her house to a point 1/2 mile, straight-line distance, from her home and observed one of these objects at a distance of 150 feet. Attached is the observer's sketch of the object seen and another drawing of the general area showing the locations of four other objects seen simultaneously. The object which she saw on 25 April 1966 was about the size of a Volkswagon car at the 150 foot range.

L. Physical Evidence: Attached are two drawings made by the observer of the object seen at close range on the night of 25 April and of the location of this and four other objects seen simultaneously and their positions relative to the observer.

So, in reality, what they tried to dismiss as a meteor, turns out to be a case of multiple sightings of several disk-shaped objects over the course of several weeks—one of which was observed at a distance of only 150 feet!

Wappingers Falls, NY, May 26, 1966

At 1:45pm, a 36-year-old housewife observed and photographed the following:

Observer watched an oblong shaped object travel toward
the western sky in about two minutes. The observer saw
red, white, and green colors during one observation.
The object left vapor trail about the same size of the
object. The object turned into a bright red ball and
disappeared. The object went straight up and disappeared.

The description is consistent with that of an aircraft
observation. The photos did not present any evidence
to indicate that an extraterrestrial vehicle.

Despite the conclusion that this was an aircraft and the photo
apparently showed nothing of an extraterrestrial nature, the file shows that
an officer at Stewart AFB has a different opinion of the case. The
following statement also shows that there were multiple eyewitnesses.
This is one of the rare instances where someone connected with Project
Blue Book admits to something possibly being of at least "unknown
origin."

J. It is my opinion that the observer could possibly have seen an object of
unknown origin. It was also noted by the observer that several people have
sighted this same object on numerous occasions in the same general areas.

Lt. J. Barnauskas, Jr.,
NAV/EWO
4713th Def Sys Eval Sq
Stewart AFB, New York

Monsey, NY, October 1, 1966

At 1:45am, a husband and wife were returning home, and when they
got out of the car they saw the following:

Observers noted football shaped, that was traveling
toward the north. Suddenly it turned NorthEast,
gathered speed and was climbing swiftly, as it was
turning two red lights seemed to come together to form
one. It suddenly hit this white object, at impact
there was a white flash, the football shaped object
shook and shuddered then it went upwards very rapidly.

The official explanation was that they probably just witnessed normal aircraft, although what's normal about a football-shaped object coming together with two other objects!? The reporting officer apparently was a bit miffed that this couple wouldn't accept his aircraft explanation, and therefore characterized them as "prejudiced witnesses."

He also wrote that, "Mr. and Mrs. X claim to be very interested in UFO Phenomena," as if there's something wrong with that. "They have seen UFOs on other occasions," which appears to be another strike against them. Finally, he writes, "They appear to be prejudiced against accepting any explanations as to what they saw that does not fit into their own experience. Neither had training that would classify them as experts in the aviation field."

This assessment made me laugh, considering the whole purpose of Project Blue Book was to assign false and misleading explanations to everything with extreme prejudice! Imagine this Air Force officer's frustration when these two people chose to believe their own eyes over his offered poor excuse?

New Rochelle, NY, October 26, 1966

This case involves a sighting by three New Rochelle policemen, who were deemed to be "very reliable witnesses." Even so, their report of a bright, round object, at an elevation of about 1,000 feet, moving "slowly from east to the south" at about 12:40am was evaluated as being "consistent with that of an aircraft."

However, in the file, the reporting officer wrote the following:

"The star Sirius was visible during this period. It had triggered several other UFO reports during this period. No other information other than reported herein could be obtained. For lack of any evidence to the contrary I believe the object in question was probably the star Sirius."

Indeed, there were reports filed from Spring Valley and Stewart AFB, both on the night of October 21, and in each case, the star Sirius was determined to be the cause. In these cases, the witnesses did say the object was stationary, so perhaps they were looking at a twinkling star. However, in the case of the three cops, they all reported that this object moved across the sky in a matter of minutes and disappeared over the horizon. That, coupled with the fact that they all estimated an elevation of 1,000 feet, and I think we can rule out Sirius. And, one would hope, that three cops wouldn't get all excited by simply watching an airplane.

Red Hook, NY, February 14, 1967

A 58-year-old electrician who was evaluated as an "exceptionally reliable witness" was three miles north of Red Hook on the night of February 14th, when he spotted a "yellowish-white" rectangle at about a 45- degree angle in a clear sky. The rectangle was at an elevation of 3,000-5,000 feet, and had "one red light 1/3 from left side. One red light center of object. Red lights were pulsating." The following sketch was drawn to illustrate what it looked like.

The object remained stationary for 45 minutes, during which time he observed it through binoculars. Then it headed west and went out of sight behind some mountains. The PBB report mentions that there was a second witness, a motel owner, who saw the same exact thing, point for point. There is also a brief mention that the object was sighted again on March 1st and 2nd.

As many of these reports do, this one contains an obvious error, most likely the result of a mistake by the reporting officer. While the electrician described the length of the object "with fingers at arm's length…at 1/8 to ¼ inch," the report also states that the shape was a "wide, rectangular strip

– 5 to 15 miles wide." Clearly, something at an elevation of 3,000-5,000 feet would blot out the sky if it was "miles wide." As the report only contains summaries of the information provided by the witnesses, and no firsthand accounts, there's no way to determine all the facts.

Suffice to say, at least two men saw a rectangular, stationary object with two red lights, for 45 minutes, which then began to move, and "due to the nature of movement, the object observed could not have been confused with an aircraft, star or planet."

However, this did not prevent the reporting officer from concluding that the witnesses simply saw the planet Venus.

New Windsor, NY, April 30, 1967

Three boys, two age 13, one 14, saw an unusual object in the sky at 5:30pm. In a handwritten letter from one the boys to Wright Patterson AFB, he describes the weather as clear, the "object was solid" and "sharply outlined," had a "high pitched moderate sound" and "was in sight for two minutes." The craft was silver, and estimated to be "traveling at 18 m.p.h."

What makes this case of particular interest was that one of the boys "observed it through a camera lens" and took the following photo. Whoever wrote the letter also sketched the object's path.

Additionally, the boy writes that "Alan Hughes ran under the object," so he must have gotten a very good look at it. Unfortunately, the official report forms are not included in the file, so we don't know specifics such as the exact shape, size, etc., but even with the poor quality of the reproduced image some of those details can be estimated.

Surprisingly, the PBB conclusion did not attempt to explain this away as an aircraft or weather balloon. However, even with the eyewitness testimony of three people, one of whom was directly underneath the craft, and the photograph, the case was dismissed on the basis of "Insufficient Data for Evaluation."

Walker Valley, NY, May 3, 1967

This case does not provide the most compelling evidence, but I am including it for two reasons. First, it takes place in Walker Valley, which is adjacent to Pine Bush, one of the most active UFO areas of the Hudson Valley. Secondly, because of the scolding the reporting officer received for shoddy work.

Mrs. Kemp was a 33-year-old "salesgirl and housewife," and on the evening of May 3, 1967, she noticed a bright red flashing light while looking out her kitchen window at her house on Route 52. It looked "round but flat—dome on top," and it appeared to be stationary in the northwestern sky for about an hour. When it started to move, she tried to follow it in her car, but lost it. A short time after returning home, the

143

object appeared again in the same area, but disappeared from view after a few minutes.

At the end of the report it states that her "Estimate of Reliability" was quite good: "Seemed level-headed and reliable. Husband and three sons also saw it." One would have thought that the fact that this was a sighting involving five witnesses would have been mentioned earlier and more prominently, but that was obviously not the only shortcoming of the report.

The following was part of a letter sent to Major Lennis Harris from Colonel James Manatt, Director of Technology and Subsystems, requesting that the report be redone with more clarification.

"The information in this report is not only confusing but worthless as a tool for evaluating a UFO sighting. Specific and detailed information is needed when filling out a UFO report. It is quite apparent that someone went through the motions of filling out the report without giving much thought to its content."

Even though it seemed like Col. Manatt was taking this case seriously, ultimately, the conclusion was just another "sweep it under the carpet" dismissal, although they decided to use two different explanations in their official bag of excuses. According to the summary form, what the Kemp family first saw was the planet Venus. The second object was a helicopter.

The Venus/Helicopter conclusion was drawn, even though Manatt included the following in the report:

"Mrs. Kemp stated that she thought people were imagining things when they reported anything like this and she hesitated a long time before she reported this to Stewart AFB. I asked if she had seen a Helicopter and she replied that this was her first thought but decided it couldn't be since there was no sound."

11
Northern New Jersey, 1962

Over the years, there have been many UFO sightings in northern New Jersey—sightings that have sometimes begun or ended in the Hudson Valley. Thanks to numerous newspaper articles and Project Blue Book and NICAP reports, we can examine one of the most prolonged waves of New Jersey sightings, which began in West Nyack, NY on the evening of September 15, 1962, and continued until September 28.

September 15
- West Nyack, NY: At 6pm, J.J. McVicker, a former Navy officer, saw two disk-shaped craft overhead, looking like "silver dollars."
- Oradell Reservoir, NJ: At 7:55pm, three boys saw a silent round object, with fins on the top and bottom, descend from treetop level toward the water near the Oradell Avenue dam. It landed on the surface of the water and made a loud splashing sound. It submerged briefly, and then ascended and accelerated at a high rate of speed, disappearing from sight to the south. As it passed overhead, it was at an altitude of about 500 feet. Shortly after, as the boys were reporting the incident to the police, Patrolman Walla noted that they "were out of breath and appeared to be very frightened" by what they witnessed. Walla called the Operations Officer at McGuire Air Force Base, and he was "very interested" in the sightings and "took a full report."
- The Haworth police department reported that several men working on the reservoir witnessed the same craft and heard the splash at the same time.
- Two other boys who were fishing saw a bright light moving back and forth along the edge of the reservoir and then heard the splash.
- Two additional witnesses saw the craft, which was moving toward the reservoir. Other witnesses described a glowing object the size of a small plane.

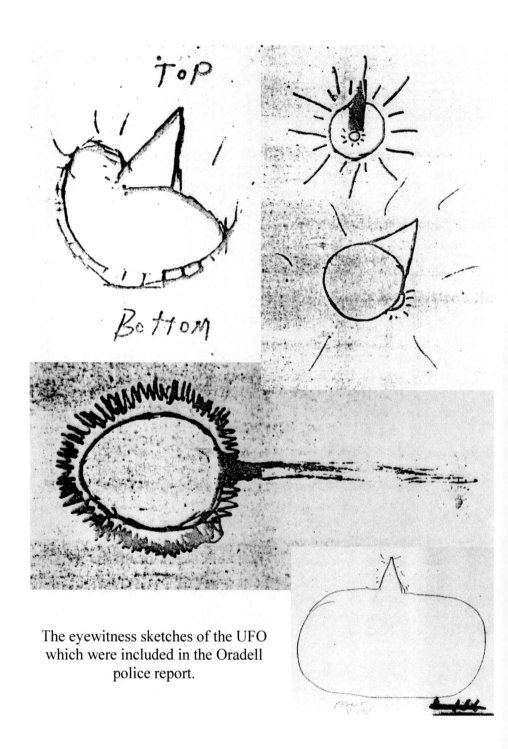

The eyewitness sketches of the UFO which were included in the Oradell police report.

- Some of the boys pointed out the object to a man at the reservoir. According to the police report, upon seeing the craft the man "ran, very fast, in the opposite direction."
- Emerson, NJ: Bizarre "banana-shaped tracks" were found at the site where several people witnessed the craft landing, before the Oradell sightings began. The Air Force immediately sent someone to investigate, and the police were then instructed to "barricade" the property to prevent the public from approaching the site.

Remarkably, the official Project Blue Book conclusion of all the September 15 sightings was—are you ready for this?—birds! Yes, it's hard to believe, but despite the numerous eyewitnesses, the sketches, the lights, the size, the movement, and the barricading of an apparent landing site, Project Blue Book, in its infinite wisdom, decided it was nothing more than birds! It then admits there was "No attempt at analysis of many other rptd (reported) sightings" which occurred over the next two weeks.

PROJECT 10073 RECORD CARD

1. DATE	2. LOCATION		12. CONCLUSIONS
15-24 September 1962	Oradell, New Jersey		☐ Was Balloon ☐ Probably Balloon ☐ Possibly Balloon
3. DATE-TIME GROUP	4. TYPE OF OBSERVATION		☐ Was Aircraft ☐ Probably Aircraft ☐ Possibly Aircraft
Local ___ GMT __15/2345Z__	x☒ Ground-Visual ☐ Air-Visual	☐ Ground-Radar ☐ Air-Intercept Radar	
5. PHOTOS ☐ Yes ☒ No	6. SOURCE Civilian		☐ Was Astronomical ☐ Probably Astronomical ☐ Possibly Astronomical
7. LENGTH OF OBSERVATION not reported	8. NUMBER OF OBJECTS one	9. COURSE south	☒x☒Other__Birds___ ☐ Insufficient Data for Evaluation ☐ Unknown
10. BRIEF SUMMARY OF SIGHTING Round obj w/fin on top & bottom. Body 4 times as large as fins. Size of piper cub at 3/4 miles. No color. Bright lights around body. Moving N to S along Oradell Reservoir. First observed over tree, obj hovered, then moved South, hovered & dropped into water. It rose about 500 ft as it passed obsrvrs. Disappeared heading S. Obsrvd fm bridge. Obsvation at night-calm water, clear moon. (See Case File)		11. COMMENTS This sighting triggered a flurry of rptd sightings fm the N.J. area fm 15-24 Sep. Carried in most UFO publications. Analysis of this particular sighting is based on limited data presented. Case evaluated as birds until further data submitted indicating other evaluation. No attempt at analysis of many other rptd sightings.	

ATIC FORM 329 (REV 26 SEP 52)

147

September 16
- Emerson, NJ: Two boys reported seeing a domed craft with two "portholes" descend behind some pine trees, then heard a sound much louder than "a car door slamming." The police contacted the boys' parents and told them that the boys should not speak about what they saw, as the government had requested secrecy.

September 18
- Westwood, N J: At 4am, a huge craft was seen by two policemen. They described it as being like an inverted cone shape.
- Oradell, NJ: At 4:45 am two other policeman saw a very bright light in the sky.
- Hawthorne, NJ: At 7:55 pm, multiple eyewitnesses in the same family reported a green disk over their house.
- Neptune City, NJ:

Patrolmen Report ✕
Sky Lights PART OF N W J

At 5:30 a. m. on 18 September 1962, Officers James Dugan of Neptune City, New Jersey, saw two strange "gigantic" lights in the sky. He spotted the lights while driving in his patrol car, then raced to headquarters where Officer Lawrence Leming was on desk duty. Leming went outside the building with Dugan and also saw the lights. Dugan estimated they were "about a mile apart," and hovered over the borough for a while. When Leming saw them they were traveling fast and heading out over the ocean, where they eventually disappeared.

An article included in the Project Blue Book file. Handwritten note at top reads "Part of New Jersey Flap."

September 20

- Emerson, NJ: Witnesses claim that three fighter jets headed straight for a brilliantly illuminated, disk-shaped craft over the reservoir. They passed underneath it, and as they turned to make another pass, the craft rose straight up and out of sight.
- Hawthorne, NJ:

Disc Illuminates Area

William Stock of Lodi, N. J., was making a routine check of the grounds at Sam Braen's Quarry, 562 Goffle Road, on Thursday, 20 September, when he sighted a round, disc-shaped object suspended in the air which lighted up the entire area. When he beamed the lights of his jeep at the object, it bobbed up and down and from side to side and then turned around. "As it turned around, I could see what appeared to be headlights. It then disappeared very fast," Stock said. No further details, but this is one more of many sightings of objects near water deposits.

An article included in the Project Blue Book file.

September 21

- Hawthorne, NJ: Between 3:40am and 4:00am, William Stock and four cops watch a hovering, round craft with lights that changed colors. One of the officers, George Jediny, sketched

149

the disk-shaped object in his NICAP report. Two additional policemen in the area see the object for approximately 35 minutes.

- Hawthorne, NJ: Four people see a bright object with beams of light emanating from it.
- Hackensack, and East Paterson, NJ: Six bright objects are witnessed in daylight at Pulaski Park in Hackensack. That night, 200 people on top of Garret Mountain in East Paterson see the same objects.
- Newark, Hasbrouck, Emerson, and other north New Jersey locations: Due to a flurry of reports that night, a reporter from the Newark office of the New York Herald Tribune set out at 11pm. He witnessed four craft shaped like "top hats" that were brightly illuminated with blue-white lights, with a red light on top. He interviewed many other witnesses, including four cops in Emerson. The sightings lasted 1.5 hours throughout northern New Jersey. He reported the sightings to McGuire AFB, and was informed that "they would look into it in the morning." The official Project Blue Book explanation was that all of the sightings were mirages caused by a temperature inversion.

The reporter's sketch of one of the four objects he witnessed.

September 23

- Hawthorne, NJ: In broad daylight, a Mrs. Lee and her son on Emeline Drive, witnessed a silver, cigar-shaped craft. It approached their location, then turned 90 degrees and sped off.

September 24

- Hawthorne, NJ: Early that morning, a group of people saw an object changing colors for 10 minutes. The group included George Della Penta, chief reporter of the New Jersey State Press, and over a dozen policemen. Della Penta filmed the object, which moved off when one of the cops aimed a spotlight at it. Later that night, another policeman saw a light hovering for 15 minutes before it moved off.

September 28

- Hawthorne, NJ: Between 2:30am and 3:30am, three color-changing UFOs are reported by the police.

Despite all the many pages in the Project Blue Book files and the many calls to McGuire AFB, the following is the response given to someone seeking information about this important wave of sightings:

29 November 1962

Dear Mr. Laval:

The sightings to which you refer in your letter of October 11th have never been officially reported to the Air Force according to our files. Therefore we are not able to effect an evaluation.

Sincerely,

WILLIAM J. LOOKADOO
Lt. Colonel, USAF
Public Information Div
Office of Information

A 2013 Google Earth image of the Oradell Reservoir with the surrounding towns of Oradell, Emerson, and Haworth. Obviously, the area has developed a great deal since the 1962 sightings.

12
The Best for Last?

One beautiful Saturday in August of 2013, my husband, Bob Strong, and I, went to a garage sale on Orange Turnpike in Monroe, NY. As it turned out, he had known the owners of the house, Nancy and Dale Forsberg, since high school.

Nancy and Dale knew I had written *In the Night Sky*, and happened to mention that Orange Turnpike was a hotbed of UFO activity over the years. They wondered if I had any interest in hearing about all the sightings. Also, they just might have a piece of physical evidence involved with one of the craft having landed on their property—if I wanted to see it.

Well, to paraphrase, you could have knocked me over with an extraterrestrial feather!

The surprises didn't end there, however. When Bob and I went back to their house a few days later to conduct the interview, we discovered there was another sighting to discuss, and on the same street and in the same town as the DiLalla case I wrote about in *In the Night Sky*.

It was 1983, and the Forsbergs were living at 72 South Harrison Avenue in Congers, NY. (That house has since been demolished.) It was the end of June, and their 11-year-old son was at a friend's house on Rockland Avenue, just the next street over, at an end-of-school party. It was between 9-10pm, when he called his parents to tell them to look outside because there was a UFO.

"I grabbed my binoculars and we ran outside," Dale explained. "There were five white lights in a triangle shape and they were moving south very slowly, maybe 15 miles per hour."

He said that even though they could only see the lights, it appeared to be a single object, and it was low in the sky, moving just above Trap Rock mountain and the hills by Rockland Lake.

"It was moving so slowly and silently, and then *whoosh*, another light came speeding up from behind so fast! The light shot forward and looked as though it went inside the object, because it was gone."

153

While Dale stayed home and watched the object through the binoculars, Nancy went to pick up their son, and remained to watch the object with everyone at the party.

"We watched it for a long time," Nancy recalls, "and a lot of people saw it."

The object finally moved to the south and out of sight. Dale later spoke to people in Westchester who saw the same thing that night. There were also many other witnesses in the area, and there must have been enough calls to the police that the incident appeared in the newspaper the next day.

"There was an article in the *Journal News* that said it was a formation of ultralights," Dale said with disgust, and then added, "That's complete BS! This was *not* a formation of planes."

What is it about this small town of Congers, that it has been the site of so many sightings, as well as abductions, dating back to at least the 1950s? I wish I knew, but I do know my research uncovered so many cases that Congers got its own chapter in *In the Night Sky*! And what are the chances that when the Forsbergs left Congers, they moved to another hotspot of UFO activity?

After moving to their home on Orange Turnpike in 1996, they began hearing stories from neighbors, and they didn't just involve lights in the sky.

One story occurred about 1969. The previous owners were awakened around midnight by someone frantically banging on their front door. They went to see what was wrong, and there on their doorstep, was a couple, scared out of their minds and nearly hysterical. They claimed that they had followed a UFO all the way from Tuxedo (or had *it* followed *them*?), and that it had just landed in the field next to the house.

The Forsbergs weren't sure what happened next, but at this point, a neighbor, Donna MacGuire, came over. Not only did she have more information about this story, but she had other stories to share, as well as one of the most remarkable photos I've seen. She was able to inform us that the previous owners of the Forsbergs' house did see the UFO that had landed by their house, and were so alarmed that they called the State Police! Whether or not the police did anything is unknown, but given their track record in such matters, it's doubtful they even responded.

Donna also related that another neighbor, who grew up on Orange Turnpike, told her that everyone along the street had sightings throughout the 1970s. In fact, the entire neighborhood had a lot of activity for many years, and there was more than one craft that had actually landed.

The most remarkable encounter, however, was the one Donna personally experienced, and photographed. It was late at night sometime in 1982, when suddenly "there were these bright lights shining in the bedroom window, as if a Mack truck had just pulled up."

Donna explained that their house was at the end of a very long driveway, so it wasn't possible for car headlights from the road to illuminate their bedroom.

They had two large, Samoyed dogs who "started going crazy" as if there were intruders.

"I tried waking up my husband, but I couldn't get him to wake up. And usually, I was frantic at the thought of someone possibly breaking in, but for some reason, I just said, 'You know what, I don't care if someone breaks in.' That was so unlike me, and it doesn't make any sense now, but I just wanted to go to sleep. I didn't care what was happening."

The next thing she knew, it was morning. She told her husband what had happened, and as a science teacher, he thought it was nonsense. However, he went outside to see if there was any sign that something had been there, "and came back in shock."

They had been working on a building project on the house, and had a truckload of sand delivered in the driveway to use to make concrete. It had been a huge pile, but now it was all gone, blown away, and in its place were several concentric circles literally melted into the blacktop!

Clearly, something circular had landed in their driveway where the pile of sand had been, blowing it away in all directions. Even after trying to brush away the circles, they remained, as if the sand had been fused or pressed into the pavement. And the circles were there for many years, until they had the driveway repaved.

Fortunately, they had the presence of mind to take photographs that day. The outermost circle was approximately 12 feet in diameter. For comparison and to give some sense of scale, one of the photos shows the back of their car.

Donna's formerly skeptical husband immediately called the State Police, who didn't seem interested and never even came over to take a report. He then called the Air Force, which also took no action. He tried making several other calls, but no one seemed interested, and he finally said he didn't know who else to call. They later found out that the police and Air Force had "been inundated with calls," so they were unable to take reports and respond to all of them.

Their loss in this case! What could they have discovered if they had taken samples of the circles in Donna's driveway? (And don't think I haven't thought of taking a pick and shovel over there and seeing if the old surface is still under the new blacktop!)

Their son, at the time, was four years old, and as they discussed the circles—never mentioning UFOs or aliens—he shouted, "ET was here! ET was here!" A child's imagination, or did he see more than lights that night?

Also, why did Donna have the strong urge to just go to sleep at such a time, when something was lighting up her bedroom brighter than daylight, and the dogs were barking hysterically?

This was obviously some sort of close encounter, but just how close we may never know.

"They call Pine Bush the hotbed of sightings," Donna said with a smile, "but I felt like there was a party in my yard that night!"

Donna then mentioned what the Forsbergs had found when they first moved in, which brought us back full circle, so to speak.

Soon after moving in, Dale and Nancy noticed an area where the tree branches were all bent and broken, looking as though they had been blasted upward, and the trees were all black as if they had been burned. Standing in the center of this anomaly, they could see it was circular, and about 15 feet in diameter. Clearly, something round and solid had lifted up from the ground at this point, snapping tree limbs upward as it took off.

While Dale always thought that UFOs could exist, he never fully believed it as much as he did the day he stood in the midst of that circle. Realizing this could be something very special, he removed a large piece of the blackened bark. For 17 years, he kept that piece of bark in the garage. I was hoping that he might give me a small piece of that bark so I could try to get it tested, and imagine how thrilled I was when he gave me the entire piece! This could be hard evidence of UFOs in the Hudson Valley!

After so many years of exposure to the elements, and sitting in a garage, I realized the chances of finding chemical anomalies were slim, but if there was any chance, it was worth a try. After all, it's not every day you get to hold a piece of evidence from a UFO landing site!

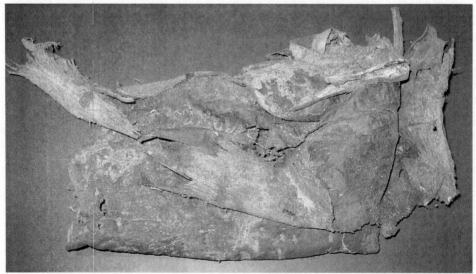

The large piece of bark.

I contacted chemist Phyllis Budinger, who is very well known for examining evidence on many famous cases, including Betty Hill's dress, and soil samples from the site of a landed craft in Delphos, Kansas. She kindly agreed to test the bark, so I cut off some pieces and sent them to her lab.

I waited on pins and needles for about a week, when I got the results. Unfortunately, there were no alien compounds. The blackish substance was a type of fungus, and the whitish deposits were composed of calcium oxalate, which is also naturally occurring. It was somewhat disappointing, but it's always best to have the facts rather than continue to indulge in speculation.

Of course, this doesn't mean that some type of extraterrestrial craft didn't land on that spot where Dale got the bark, it simply means that it either left no residue, or it was washed away over the years.

So, what is it about Orange Turnpike in Monroe that attracts so much UFO activity? I could ask the same thing about Congers, Pine Bush, Peekskill, Brewster, Poughkeepsie, Kingston, Saugerties, and Albany. In fact, I could ask that question for the entire Hudson Valley and northern New Jersey.

For over 100 years, something has been in our skies, landing in our fields and forests, and making our residents lose time and experience physical and emotional trauma. The evidence is there—from eyewitness testimony, to photos and video, to tangible pieces of something having visited us.

Is the Hudson Valley the #1 Hotspot for UFO activity in the country? Taking into account the number of sightings, the intensity of the experiences, and the long history of reports, I am convinced it is.

What do you think?

Special Addition

The following did not take place in the Hudson Valley,
so consider this chapter a "bonus feature."

Heights of Strangeness

Jon Betancourt, Chicago Heights, IL

At the 2013 Pine Bush UFO Festival, a man started telling me about some of the experiences he and his family have had since he was a child in Chicago Heights, Illinois. Even though these events did not take place locally, he is now a resident of the Hudson Valley—in fact, by coincidence (or not!) he lives just minutes from downtown Pine Bush. His stories were so compelling I wanted to interview him, so I asked how I could get in touch with him.

"I work with your husband," Jon said, much to my surprise, once again proving what a small world it is.

We arranged for me to come to his house, where he lives with his wife, Susan, and their young son. The stories I heard over the next couple of hours went to prove that just when you think you can't stretch the bizarre UFO envelope any further, your mind can still be blown. I don't know what it is about this area of Illinois, but like Pine Bush, Putnam County, and other places in the Hudson Valley, it appears to be a ground zero for what Dr. J. Allen Hynek called "high strangeness."

With so much strangeness to cover, we decided to just start from the beginning and go chronologically, which brought us to one night around 1980 when Jon was about 7 years old. His mother, Balbina, was in the kitchen, and he distinctly remembers her asking if he wanted to go outside and "see the light in the sky." They went out in the yard with Jon's older brother, who was about 17, and there was indeed something bright up in the sky—only it was a lot more than just a light.

"It was like an upside down crown," Jon explained. "It was round on top, then there were these sticks or stalks coming down that had red, green, and white lights on the end of them. The body of the object looked black, and there were rotating lights around it, or it was spinning."

He doesn't know at what altitude it was hovering, but he knew it was huge. Oddly, no one was frightened by the object. They all just stood and stared "with a sense of wonderment, trying to figure out what it was." It moved slightly, but kept the same general position in the sky. Today, with his knowledge of astronomy, he knows it was high in the sky, between the Little Dipper and the zenith. At the same time, with his knowledge of planes and all things in the night sky, he knows without a doubt it was something very unusual.

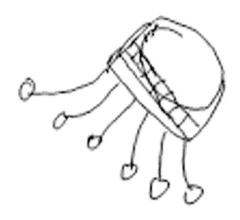

And it got even stranger, as the craft appeared several more times over the course of a week. Each time it hovered overhead, he and his mother and brother would stand outside and watch this

Jon's sketch of the crown-like craft.

bizarre craft. Then it stopped appearing, and Jon "didn't pay much attention" to UFOs or other peculiar phenomena until 1991, when he was about 19.

It was the middle of the night and he was sound asleep. His mother shook him awake and said, "Someone is outside."

He could hear that the family's big Samoyed dog was in the yard barking, and he assumed that the dog would deter anyone from going onto their property, so he told his mother not to worry. He was going to lay down again to go back to sleep, but his mother grabbed his shoulders, looked right into his eyes, and in an urgent tone he had never heard before, she insisted, *"Get up now!"* Even with this uncharacteristic behavior from his mother, Jon wasn't too alarmed, as the neighborhood wasn't what it had once been, and vagrants often went across the field behind their house and into the adjacent woods, but he decided to humor her.

He went to his window and saw the dog on its hind legs barking and straining to get at someone, or something, but that's all he could see. Then they went into the next room which had a better view of the field.

"Look, it's right there. He's right there, look!" his mother said in an excited, but low voice.

Jon still didn't see anything until he looked toward a large tree in the field about 100 yards from the house. Then he did see something, but was in "complete disbelief" about what he saw.

"There was a shimmering figure, glowing white, almost electric. It looked like white fur standing up on its arms, legs, and body, almost like static," Jon said thoughtfully, still trying to figure out what he had witnessed over 20 years ago. "It was pacing, it wasn't alarmed, just walking around a few feet away from the tree."

The field behind the house and the large tree where Jon first spotted the figure. The crosses were part of a series of sculptures depicting the Stations of the Cross.

After a while, it "walked out into ankle-high grass, and it was human walking, but its arms were very long and its whole body was shimmering. Everything was lit up around him like two bright, LED flashlights. I almost expected the grass or the trees to catch fire. It was just so difficult to wrap my head around what I was seeing!"

At this point, his mother was going to go into another room to see if she could get a better look.

"I grabbed her by the wrist and said, 'You're not leaving me! I don't know how tall that thing is, but I guarantee it can walk up to this window and look right in at me!'"

With that thought, Jon was scared for the first time since he began watching this glowing figure, as it brought up a lifelong fear that someone was looking in the window at him. He always had the unnerving feeling that he wasn't alone in that house. In retrospect, he may have been right!

After watching the figure for at least fifteen minutes, it "faced the house, crossed its legs, and sat down in the grass. The grass all around him was lit up, and you could see his arms stretch out grabbing pieces of grass, like he was playing or just curious."

The glowing figure sat there for about ten minutes, and all the while Jon was thinking, "Please don't see me!" When the figure stood up, it walked toward the woods, which were about 30 feet away, but didn't go far into the tree line, and then it came back into the field near the tree. For another long period of time—at least 20 minutes—the figure just walked back and forth across the field and in and out of the woods. Studying its movements and seeing it at all angles, Jon could see that proportionately, it looked human—except for its large size, and the glowing white light, of course!

Finally, it again walked toward the tree line, and according to Jon's mother (who I interviewed a few weeks later), the figure just disappeared. Remarkably, the total time Jon watched this thing was 45 minutes! Even more remarkably, his mother had been watching it at least another 30 minutes before she woke him up. And while she was watching it, it was in a different part of the field, near church property where there was a large semi-circle of statues known as the Stations of the Cross.

This is probably a good point to talk a little about the history of this land. It is near the old Sauk Trail, a Native American pathway through Illinois, Indiana, and Michigan. There had once been many Indian villages in the area. Fast forward to the late 1800s, when immigrants from Italy came to this area of Chicago Heights, and they built a Catholic church in

1906. This neighborhood became known as Hungry Hill, because these immigrants were so poor, they ate out of trash cans.

Balbina told me that when they first moved to this house in the late 1970s, the neighborhood was exclusively Italian, except for one other family. She learned that the woman who previously owned the house made spaghetti for a local restaurant. One day, Al Capone came to her door and wanted to know if he could store some things at her house! She must have been a very brave woman, because she said no, as she didn't want people coming in and out with all the spaghetti drying on racks all around the house.

Capone was not happy with her refusal, and one can only wonder what it was he wanted to store (bootleg liquor, guns?), and why he chose this house. This woman was just lucky that her refusal to the infamous mob boss didn't cost her life, as the people in the pharmacy a block away were not so lucky—they were all gunned down.

Balbina also told me that the church field had once been a junkyard full of abandoned cars. Apparently, not all of those abandoned cars were empty, though, as the junkyard became a popular place to dump bodies. Today in this area, people are afraid of all the Latin gangs and claim it is too dangerous to live here, but it doesn't sound like it was the safest place to live in the days of Al Capone and the junkyard, either!

There was one other piece of information that Balbina shared that brought up an interesting question. One summer, late at night, several cars pulled up and parked along the street. Then people got out dressed in long, black, hooded robes. They went back to the area of the statues and then after a while, they went back to their cars and took off. This happened numerous times, but Balbina believes they stopped coming because they either realized they were being watched, or someone reported them to the church or police.

Were they Pagans, Wiccans, members of a secret society, or devil worshippers? Why did the come to this particular field? If this was meant as some sort of protest or snub to the Catholic Church, why do it in the middle of the night when they didn't think anyone was looking?

And if the presence of the church statues had nothing to do with these gatherings, then what was it about this particular field that drew them here? Was this allegedly a place sacred to the Native Americans? Had the activity here given it the reputation for having unique energies? Normally,

I wouldn't think twice about a bunch of people running around in robes, but in lieu of the UFOs, glowing figures, murders, and other bizarre activity (there are many, many accounts of haunted activity, but that's another story), I can't help but wondering why these people went out of their way to gather at the dead of night on this spot.

Getting back to the glowing figure, when Jon got home from school the next day, he and his mother went back onto the field to look for signs of the night visitor. Having grown up playing in the nearby woods, he was used to seeing all sorts of animal tracks, and fully expected to find some huge tracks in the soft soil. However, as carefully as he looked, he couldn't find a single footprint anywhere, which just seemed impossible. But there was one incredible thing he discovered.

While tracing the approximate path the figure took through the high grass, Jon heard his mother calling to him, asking where he was. He turned to respond and realized he couldn't see her, because the grass was at least six feet high and over his head. Yet, when the figure was walking through this same grass, he could see it from the chest up—meaning it had to be nine or ten feet tall!

I honestly didn't know what to make of this level of strangeness, but it didn't end there. In October of 1992, Jon's mother once again woke him up in the middle of the night and said, "It's back."

"What!?" Jon asked, trying to fathom what she was saying.

"There's something out there again."

"Is it the same thing?"

"You need to come look at this," was all she would say.

Jumping out of bed and running to the window, he expected to see the big, glowing figure under the tree, but he didn't see anything. Then his mother told him to look *in the tree*. With the street and church lights helping to illuminate the field, Jon did indeed catch sight of something in a tree—a black figure standing on a limb, with its arms above its head holding on to another branch. Then the figure started moving in a swaying motion, kind of bouncing up and down on the limb.

"Do you see it?" his mother asked.

"You mean the *black thing*?" he replied, not knowing what to call it. "I...don't know what it is. I'm still trying to figure out what we saw last year!"

Of course, it would get even stranger. The figure let go of the branch above it, and looked like it was about to jump.

"Then there was this blue flash, and suddenly it was in another tree!"

The black figure was now 20 feet away, and Jon was clear that it didn't physically leap over to the other tree—there had been a deep, cobalt blue flash of light, and it disappeared from the first tree and appeared in the second. Then there was another blue flash, and it was in a third tree— and so on until the black figure had gone at least 100 yards from tree to tree.

I asked if he took any photos this time.

"We had an 8mm camera in the house, *but I could not leave that window*. People don't understand, but if you are ever in that same situation, you let me know how you react."

This was a life-altering experience, in more ways than one, as his career as a pro-am photographer began that night.

"From that day I always made it a point to carry a camera. *You have to have a camera with you*," he emphasized. "You've got to have proof that you saw what you saw."

I asked if this figure was as big as the first one, and Jon said it was smaller—about seven feet. I guess smaller is a relative term when talking about these things!

Once this black figure reached the tree line it jumped—or more correctly flashed—down to the ground and walked in the same area the previous glowing figure had walked the year before. Jon and his mother could now get a better look as it was out of the trees, but if they were hoping they would be able to identify it, they were mistaken, as the figure also looked like it had a tail!

A natural reaction would be to assume that a monkey had escaped the zoo or it was someone's pet on the loose—but there were no reports of 7-foot-tall fugitive monkeys, and no species of monkey are known to be able to transport themselves with blue flashes of light. Jon's mother couldn't say what this was they saw, she could only say "it didn't belong here."

This time, the sighting "only lasted about 20 minutes," which made me laugh. In a field where a 2-second glimpse of something can be mind-blowing, I just couldn't conceive of such a prolonged experience by two people, for the second time in a year. And there would be other people who would see "a glowing thing" in that field over the next few years.

At this point I sincerely wish I could offer the reader some rational explanation for any of this, but I really don't know what to make of it all, so I'm just a reporter here! And there's more to report.

This time it was the summer of 1993, and Jon was at a club in Chicago with a friend, and the friend's girlfriend. He made it clear that they weren't old enough to drink, and had only had soda and juice all night. On the way back to Chicago Heights, Jon was sitting in the back seat of a 1989 Thunderbird, which had a long, sloping back window.

They were on State Street, heading towards Route 30, and had just gone over a set of railroad tracks and were approaching another set when Jon noticed a bright light behind them.

"There were six cars on the road; us, and five other cars. Three to our left, and two in front of us. My friend, who was driving, said, 'What the f--- is that!?' His girlfriend also said, 'What is that!?' I asked who had their f'ing brights on. I turned around to look out the back, and there was no car behind us, but it is white around us, it is very lit up."

He turned back to see the car to his left, a green Tempo with tan interior, which was also lit up so brightly he could see the car and driver as clear as if it was daylight, and he recognized the driver as a girl he knew.

"And this is a very dark road, and it's 2 o'clock in the morning. Then my friend looked up through the sunroof and said again, 'What the f--- is that!?' I leaned my head back so I could look up, and above us was a round craft with large domes of light beneath it. In the center was the largest dome, and around it were lights that were red, white, green. There were six lights. In the middle was white, and it was large, *and it was very low!* I would say *maybe* 150 feet off the ground. It lit up all the cars.

"I couldn't believe what I was looking at, and the tears just started running down out of my eyes. It was silver metallic, the bottom of it. I couldn't see the top."

I asked Jon if could estimate the diameter of the craft, and he replied that was easy. He went on to discuss the dimensions of the road at that location in a manner that didn't sound like a typical motorist. He must have seen my puzzled expression, and explained that he used to do land surveying, so distances and dimensions were second nature. Long story short, the craft was about 60 feet in diameter.

When they were only about a block from where they had to turn, "the light got so intense I had to duck down and cover my eyes." He then made a combination of a humming and whirring sound, and said that the craft made that sound "like it was powering up. And then all of a sudden it streaked straight south. It went so fast it turned into a streak of light. And then on the horizon, over the town of Crete, there were these flashes of light, green and red and orange, like something exploded. At that point I almost really lost it. I really had tears coming down my eyes."

His friend declared, "That's it, I'm going home!"

Jon begged him to follow it, but his friend's response was, "F--- you, I'm dropping you off, and I'm going home." When Jon got out of the car he was shaking, and he sat up for the longest time trying to process what they had just seen before he was able to go to bed.

"From that point I started paying a lot more attention to what was going on around me! I just know that whatever I saw wasn't from around here. It wasn't ours, it wasn't theirs, it was somebody else's."

Over the years, Jon has tried to discuss the experience with his friends, but they have both repeatedly said that they don't want

Jon's sketch of the round, lighted craft.

to. In fact, it was so distressing they *never* want to talk about it again.

Next in the order of events came Susan's sighting in 1996. She was now living in the house, and at the time was smoking. It was a cool night, "sweatshirt weather." Jon was at a friend's house, and Susan went outside to have a cigarette. Lights in the sky caught her attention, and she looked up to see a large "arrowhead or boomerang-shaped" craft above the area of the Stations of the Cross.

The craft wasn't very low, but as it hung motionless and silent, she could clearly see blue, round lights, none of which were flashing. She stared at this craft for about 15-20 minutes—more than enough time for the cigarette to burn her fingers because she was so mesmerized she forgot she was holding it!

She thought about running inside for a camera, but she was afraid it would be gone when she came back out. At some point, the lights changed from all blue to all white. Eventually, it just "shot off" and a very high rate of speed.

"I wasn't scared," Susan replied to my question of how she felt during the sighting. "I was just curious as to what it could be. I knew it wasn't a plane or anything else I had ever seen. And I know planes. I grew up by Midway [Airport]. My mom and I would go to White Castle and sit on the hood of the car and watch the planes."

"I know from my experiences of seeing planes and blimps and what have you, and that's *not* what I saw. There were no flashing lights and it was fast, *really fast,* like whoosh, but no sound."

I was surprised to learn that Jon had never told Susan about any of his experiences, so she could not have been influenced by his stories. It wasn't until she told him about her sighting that night that he began sharing his.

Next we go to 1998-99. The windows were open and Jon heard a loud noise one night, "like a big V-8 engine idling." Thinking it was a very unusual train, he ran outside.

"Once I got outside I realized the sound wasn't coming from street level, it was coming from the sky. So I looked straight up, it was a clear sky, and whatever it was, was maybe 300-500 feet up. It was the size of a football field, and it was clear."

"*It* was clear?" I asked, making sure we were talking about the craft and not the sky.

"*It* was clear. You could see right through it," Jon replied. "and I could actually see the stars more clearly through it, like they were magnified."

"I've heard that before," I said, thinking about Ginny's cousin near Pine Bush in January of 2013, who described that massive rectangular craft as looking like a "glass-bottomed boat."

"The only thing that differentiated it from the sky," Jon continued, "was that it was lined in red lights along the sides at every point."

He started describing the shape, and I quickly pushed my notebook toward him so he could sketch it.

Jon's sketch.

"You could see the stars through it, and at the edges you could see that light was bending. As it went past a bright star you could see it, like, shimmy. I was out there maybe 30 seconds, and I watched it go straight over the house and go west.

"At this point my dad opened the door and said, 'What was that?' I told him I didn't know. When he asked again, I said he wouldn't believe me if I told him. I was surprised he came out."

I didn't realize how unusual this was that Jon's dad came outside because of the noise, until Susan said, "Things could be blowing up and his dad would just sit there watching TV."

As for this sighting, it reminded me of a show I saw about high-tech military projects working on active (changing) camouflage, or optical (projection/reflection) camouflage. The basic technique is to have cameras taking pictures or video of what is behind an object or person, and then projecting that image on the front of that object or person who is wearing a special material. In other words, if I was standing in front of a Christmas tree, the lights, ornaments, and branches would be projected from behind onto my front, creating a type of invisibility, or at least an optical illusion that I wasn't there.

The official word is that the "technology is in a primitive stage," but what if it wasn't? What if there was some sort of blimp made with this material that projected the stars above it onto the bottom of the craft? If there hadn't been those red lights at the corners, it's likely Jon never would have seen the craft. That's some stealth technology! Whether or not it's *our* technology is the question!

We discussed this, and Jon agreed that rather than being a transparent craft, it had only the illusion of being clear and was actually solid with some sort of active/optical camouflage.

There was no major strangeness again until September of 2007, when Jon and Susan were in Oak Brook, Illinois. They were standing outside on a line for a book signing, and this time he did have his camera. He was taking pictures of planes while he waited, and noticed something that was not traveling in the normal traffic patterns for O'Hare Airport. (Jon is very knowledgeable about the runways and patterns at O'Hare.)

"At first I thought it was a balloon, or even a garbage bag caught in the wind. It was tumbling, then I noticed it was shimmering, like light bounced off of it. So still at that point I thought it was a large black bag.

"So I aimed my camera at it on the monopod, and I was trying to make sure I was keeping the path of it. I also made sure I was getting landmarks to judge distance and size."

However, the bag/balloon theory didn't hold up, as instead of quickly blowing out of site, Jon watched this object for about 20 minutes. He continued to take pictures, and finally in the last one, the object took on the form "of some sort of craft. It really shocked me." Once he got home and uploaded the images to his computer, he could see much more detail, and was convinced he had finally photographed something bizarre.

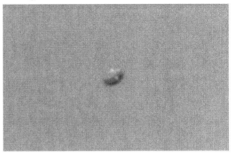

A few weeks later, Jon took a trip to California for a conference

One of Jon's photos of the object.

on solar astronomy. One night of the trip involved a visit to Mt. Wilson Observatory, where he was able to look through the massive 60-inch telescope. (Yes, I was jealous when I heard that.) When he was flying back from Los Angeles, they were passing over Mt. Wilson when he saw an object rapidly approaching the plane.

"It was a chrome, silver ball and it went right under the plane. It cleared us by maybe 50-60 feet. My camera was on my lap and I didn't even have time to pick it up. *This thing was moving fast!* I popped up out of the seat all excited, by no one else saw it."

I asked how large the object was, and Jon estimated it was about 20 feet in diameter. There were no wings, no signs of propulsion, no exhaust trail.

"It was like someone had fired a massive pinball!"

I asked if he had time to be scared, and he admitted thinking, "I hope that misses us!"

Since that incident, things have been quiet—even though Jon and Susan now live in the UFO Alley known as the Hudson Valley, near the UFO hotspot that is Pine Bush. But I suspect it's only a matter of time before I have another story or two to add to their long list of sightings.

So what do I make of all this high strangeness? Well, it's certainly not the first family to have multiple experiences by multiple family members, but it is the nature of these particular experiences that sets this case apart. Even if you tried to explain away the various UFOs as military vehicles, what do you do with the glowing figure, or the black one that moved in bursts of blue light?

To paraphrase the State Trooper that Gloria LaPolla called (See *In the Night Sky*) to report her sighting in 1984, "I'll be damned if I know what they were!"

I do think we have two separate things going on here, which are most likely related, nonetheless. The land in Chicago Heights has some weird energy that attracts everything from UFOs, to strange creatures, to people in robes conducting ceremonies.

Also, Jon and his family have some sort of connection to all of this strangeness, regardless of where they are. It does seem to be a stretch to believe that it was just a coincidence that the Betancourts just happened to live on that crazy piece of land—and that now Jon and his wife and son live near that crazy town called Pine Bush, in that crazy region of the northeast known as the Hudson Valley.

Index

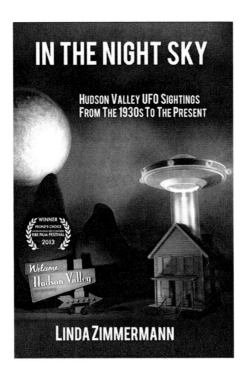

IN THE NIGHT SKY

HUDSON VALLEY UFO SIGHTINGS
FROM THE 1930S TO THE PRESENT

LINDA ZIMMERMANN

The Hudson Valley of New York has been a UFO hotspot for generations. This is the first comprehensive book to examine eyewitness accounts from the 1930s to the present. From Manhattan to Albany, people have been seeing all shapes and sizes of craft--from the giant triangles to classic flying saucers. They have also been having uncomfortably close encounters. Is the Hudson Valley also Abduction Alley?

Amazon Reviews:

➢ *I could not put the book down. One of the 3 best UFO books that I have read, and I have read a LOT.*

➢ *...stands head and shoulders above the majority of UFO books.*

➢ *You will start to read and not be able to put it down.*

IN THE NIGHT SKY
I RECALL A UFO

In The Night Sky: I Recall A UFO
the award-winning film, featuring Linda Zimmermann,
directed by Felix Olivieri, and produced by Big Guy
Media. For more information on the film and DVD
please visit:
www.nightskyufo.com

➤ Winner of the People's Choice Award at the 2013
International UFO Congress
➤ Official Selection: Hoboken International Film Festival
➤ Official Selection for the Kingston, NY Film Festival
➤ Official Selection for the Beacon, NY Film Festival

About the Author

Linda Zimmermann is a former research scientist and an award-winning author of over 30 books on science, history, and the paranormal, as well as several works of fiction (including her sentimental favorite, *Hudson Valley Zombie Apocalypse.*). She enjoys lecturing on a wide variety of topics, and has spoken at the Smithsonian Institution, Gettysburg, West Point, the Northeast Astronomy Forum, science fiction conventions, and national Mensa conventions. Linda has also made numerous appearances on radio and television.

When she isn't glued to her computer writing books, Linda goes cycling, kayaking, cross country skiing, and snowshoeing. She is a lifelong NY Mets and NY Giants fan, so don't even think of trying to call her when a game is on.

For information on all of Linda Zimmermann's publications and events:

www.gotozim.com

http://www.facebook.com/pages/Linda-Zimmermann/116636310250

www.ghostinvestigator.com
www.hvzombie.com
www.badsciences.com

Linda Zimmermann's books are available from her websites, Amazon, Barnes & Noble, and most major retailers. They are also available for Kindle, Apple, NookBook, Kobo, and other E-book formats.

Bad Science:
A Brief History of Bizarre Misconceptions, Totally Wrong Conclusions, and Incredibly Stupid Theories

Winner of the 2011 Silver Medal for Humor
in the international Independent Publisher Awards

Amazon.com Review:

"*Bad Science* is simultaneously informative and ever-so-entertaining. Riveting! Enthralling! Hilarious! I highly recommend this book if you like a jaw dropping read that is a LAUGH OUT LOUD."

HVZA:
Hudson Valley Zombie Apocalypse

Amazon.com Reviews:

"GREAT book. Buy it; you won't regret it. Well... except maybe for at 3 AM when you're either A) still up reading because can't put this page-turner down or B) waking up out of a zombie nightmare because the characters and situations in the book can seem so REAL. But buy it anyway."

"You relate, you get sucked in, seriously it's been a while since I enjoyed a book so much."

"The author has an uncanny ability to pull you into the story and make you feel like you are there."

"Zimmermann really hits home with her depiction of life during the collapse of civilization, and the heart wrenching losses, choices and sacrifices that people must make in order to survive. Zimmermann is a master manipulator of emotions: the love, fear, sadness, pain, and suffering of the various characters are surprisingly real. Set in the Hudson Valley, the authentic locations and settings lend an additional layer of realism that so many other works of fiction neglect. These just are not zombies that are attacking people - these are zombies that are attacking your neighbors and family and friends."

Dead Center
A Ghost Hunter Novel

When one of the country's largest shopping centers is built in Virginia, rumors abound that the place is haunted by ghosts of Civil War soldiers. Ghost hunter Sarah Brooks must uncover the truth, and come face to face with the restless spirits that walk through the *Dead Center*:

Okay, Sarah Brooks. This is what you do, she said to herself. *This is who you are.*

Closing her eyes, Sarah spun around and counted to three. When she opened her eyes, she had to clamp her hand over her mouth to stifle a scream. There was a pale, misty shape of a man drawing closer. It was like an image being projected into a fog, and it rippled, wavered, then slowly began to take on a more defined shape. The wounded man behind her screamed as if Death himself was coming to take him...

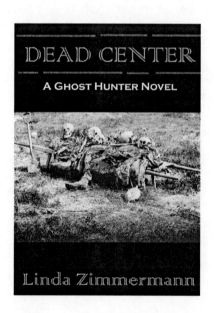

Ghost Investigator Series

Ghost Investigator Volume 1:
Hauntings of the Hudson Valley

Ghost Investigator Volume 2:
From Gettysburg to Lizzie Borden

Ghost Investigator Volume 3

Ghost Investigator Volume 4:
Ghosts of New York and New Jersey

Ghost Investigator Volume 5:
From Beyond the Grave

Ghost Investigator Volume 6:
Dark Shadows

Ghost Investigator Volume 7:
Psychic Impressions

Ghost Investigator Volume 8:
Back Into the Light

Ghost Investigator Volume 9:
Back from the Dead

Ghost Investigator Volume 10

Ghost Investigator Volume 11

Ghost Investigator 10th Anniversary Special Edition:
Favorite Haunts

Ghosts of Rockland County:
Collected Stories Edition

Hudson Valley Haunts:
Historic Driving Tours

New York's Hudson River Valley is a place of captivating beauty and fascinating history. It is also one of the most haunted regions in the country. From ancient Indian spirits at Spook Rock, to soldiers still walking the battlefield of Fort Montgomery, to the many haunted houses that line the streets of the old Dutch settlements in New Paltz and Hurley, this book has something extra to offer tourists—ghosts that still make their presence known to those who dare to visit.

What greater adventure can there be then to go to such a site, explore the rich history of its people and the events, and then see if you can discover any deeper secrets from the other world, where a passing shadow or faint whisper may signal that you have just had an encounter in the haunted Hudson Valley.

America's Historic Haunts

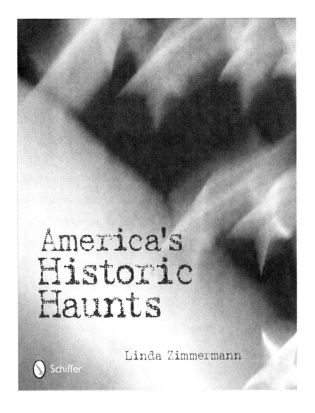

America's Historic Haunts

Linda Zimmermann

Schiffer

From remote villages in Alaska, to ancient Native American settlements in the southwest, to an old Spanish town in Florida, and bustling metropolitan areas in the northeast, follow the fascinating trail of historic haunts across the country. Test your ghost hunting skills in an old prison or fort, dine in restaurants where paranormal activity is on the menu, and sleep in some of America's most haunted inns. Whether you're a frequent flier or an armchair adventurer, this book will take you on a journey of discovery into the people, places, and events that led to the spirits that still walk among us in some of this country's greatest travel destinations.

To see the latest information on
Linda Zimmermann's projects and view her
appearance schedule go to:

www.gotozim.com